a Very Vintage HOLIDAY

COLLECTING, DECORATING, AND CELEBRATING ALL YEAR LONG

BOB RICHTER

Photography by Bud Hayman
Foreword by Christopher Radko

Globe
Pequot

Essex, Connecticut

TO EVERYONE WHO LOVES HOLIDAYS

and to those who passed that love onto us.
For me they include Mom, Dad, Nana, Grandma, Robin, Johnny, Walter,
Sharon, Sefton, Mary Margaret, Kelly, Christopher, Jay, Renee, Christina,
and Chuck. And to all the wonderful antiques dealers who rescue
vintage holiday treasures for future generations to enjoy.

THANK YOU!

Globe Pequot

An imprint of Globe Pequot, the trade division of
The Rowman & Littlefield Publishing Group, Inc.
4501 Forbes Blvd., Ste. 200
Lanham, MD 20706
www.rowman.com

Distributed by NATIONAL BOOK NETWORK

British Library Cataloguing in Publication Information available

Library of Congress Cataloging-in-Publication Data

Names: Richter, Bob, 1970– author. | Radko, Christopher, writer of foreword.
Title: A very vintage holiday : collecting, decorating and celebrating all year long / Bob Richter ; photography by Bud
  Hayman ; foreword by Christopher Radko.
Description: Essex, Connecticut : Globe Pequot, [2023] | Summary: "A celebration of all the major holidays on the
  calendar, from Easter to Halloween to Christmas—and many more. Helps the everyday collector and enthusiast make
  the most of what they've already collected and build upon it for future generations to enjoy"— Provided by publisher.
Identifiers: LCCN 2023002217 (print) | LCCN 2023002218 (ebook) | ISBN 9781493072828 (cloth) | ISBN
  9781493072835 (epub)
Subjects: LCSH: Holiday decorations. | Holidays.
Classification: LCC TT900.H6 R53 2023 (print) | LCC TT900.H6 (ebook) | DDC 745.594/16—dc23/eng/20230223
LC record available at https://lccn.loc.gov/2023002217
LC ebook record available at https://lccn.loc.gov/2023002218

♾™ The paper used in this publication meets the minimum requirements of American National Standard for
Information Sciences—Permanence of Paper for Printed Library Materials, ANSI/NISO Z39.48-1992.

TABLE of CONTENTS

A Valentine for a FINE BOY

FOREWORD

My mom had a calendar on the refrigerator door when I was a kid. She'd use it as a family reminder of upcoming appointments and events to prepare for. I noticed that some of the days were printed in red. These "red-letter days" signified something special. Even as a child, I understood that those days were meant to be festive and fun. Holidays were an escape from my humdrum life and held the promise of slowing down for good food, good times, and connections with family and friends.

While we didn't have much money for store-bought decorations, the natural world offered a cornucopia of materials to enhance our holiday decorating. For several weeks before Easter, I'd help my mom collect brown onion skins from the grocery stores. She would boil eggs in water with these skins to impart a tawny golden amber to the white shells; then she'd etch designs of flowers and bunnies on the surface. In the autumn we'd gather bright red and orange maple leaves from the park. We'd press, dry, and paste them on a large drop cloth in a spiral pattern, creating a magnificent tapestry table cover for Thanksgiving. In early December we'd take walks in a nearby woodland, collecting moss, pinecones, and twigs to create elfin buildings for the nativity under our Christmas tree. As we moved through the seasons of the year, nature was a bountiful resource for rich connections and shared memories with my mom. It warms my heart to recall how these simple crafts have enriched my life.

Bob Richter has been a wonderful part of my personal growth since he first came into my life with his book *A Very Vintage Christmas*. He reminded me that holidays, all holidays, are relevant.

I try to put a little bit of holiday into every day of my life. You can too. Bob's *A Very Vintage Holiday* shows us how. He delivers a year's worth of holidays straight into our hearts. He breathes life into each red-letter day with things we can notice, enjoy, and do, making each day a bright, beautiful memory.

Bob shows us that holidays can be turning points in our psyche and hearts, crossroads where we can creatively lift ourselves and add value to the world. Bob helps us remove the stress and put the fun back in these days. I think of this book as *holiday therapy*.

A Very Vintage Holiday is a guide to slowing down, getting present, and even healing our hearts. Bob writes that holidays allow us to appreciate the exquisite beauty of handmade decorations and the memories they contain. In slowing down to notice

the beauty, we catch our breath. And in breathing naturally again, we feel grounded and able to step into a place of heightened living. He shows us that life is well lived when we pause to find the magic in these many tiny moments of our days. So take heed. We birth beauty around us as we celebrate all our favorite holidays and welcome the rich vibe of vintage decor in our homes.

Holidays can be a tender time because we open our hearts to love. Sometimes it takes courage to connect, but holidays help pave the way. This heart warmth can also brighten all the other days of our calendar year. Sharing our holiday heart with family and friends is a way of saying "I love you." Our lives may still be imperfect, but from one holiday to the next, the joyous connections we infuse in all our days makes the world a happier place for all.

—CHRISTOPHER RADKO

Introduction
THE IMPORTANCE OF CELEBRATING HOLIDAYS

In a world where many seem to be divided, holidays have a way of bringing us together. They give us the opportunity to put our differences aside, open our hearts, connect, and be at our best. The warmth of the Christmas season, the joy of Easter, and the gratitude of Thanksgiving are annual opportunities for a renewal of sorts. In fact, I'd go so far as to say that decorating, celebrating, singing, gift-giving, and so many more activities lift our spirits and can even renew our faith in humanity.

As a kid, I knew holidays were very important in our home. They gave us something to look forward to and a special reason to be joyful. Times were not always perfect, and, like every family, we had our struggles and losses. Sometimes those hard times were happening right before a holiday, but sure enough, after dialing up some spirit, decking some halls, and opening our hearts, things were invariably better.

I collect vintage holiday items all year long and decorate for every holiday I celebrate. In most cases I use decorations that either belonged to my family or resemble ones that once did. These objects have great emotional value to me and conjure up what I refer to as the 3 Cs: Comfort, Connection, and Continuity.

The stockings my big brother Johnny made for our family now hang in my home.

Objects like the Christmas stockings my brother Johnny made for our family bring me great *comfort* because they've been part of my life for a very long time. I obviously have a great *connection* to them, as my brother made them with his own two hands and surprised us with them decades ago on a powerfully happy Christmas morning. Each time I see them, my heart is happy. The *continuity* comes from the fact that they are now in my home, as opposed to my mom's home. Some people, like my brother, have passed on, and some family members, like my partner, Sefton, have been added. So the stockings don't always go to the same person they once did, but we use them, love them, and make them relevant every year. Of course we also put an orange in the toe of each stocking, just like Mom always did.

I have examples like the stockings for just about every holiday, and I'll share them with you. Chances are, you'll relate and have your own versions of these wonderful vintage ways. A few include wearing a new outfit to church on Easter Sunday, creating handmade Valentine's cards, and pressing leaves and decorating with them for Thanksgiving. Did you do these things? I sure did—and I still do. These are family traditions. And traditions really help unite us on holidays throughout the year.

Those vintage ways and traditions extend to cooking and baking, of course, and I'm really excited to include some of Mom's recipes for holiday favorites like her pineapple filling for Easter or her spiced tongue cookies for Halloween. The smell of these things cooking in my home brings back a floodgate of memories and is a treat for the senses.

We were also a very crafty family, and by the age of seven, I was making Christmas ornaments with my mom. I still have them, and as I grow older, they have become more and more valuable to me. We also made decorations for Easter, and most other holidays. The same went for gifts. I learned to sew and quill, and I even made hair combs for my sister. I also made framed creations

Here I am experiencing what I call "tree glee" on my fourth Christmas. This is the tree my big brother Johnny created for me as a surprise. I still have the ornaments and the Santa.

for all family members. Many of them are still hanging on their walls.

While I don't make as many decorations and gifts today, I always manage to do some. Similarly, I am always grateful when I receive someone's handmade or home-baked creation. To me, they are the greatest gifts of all. They represent time and creativity—and that person's hands were literally in every bit of the item's creation.

At the same time I started making ornaments and gifts, I began to collect vintage decorations I found at auctions and charity sales with my dad. This was after Dad gave me a beautiful box of vintage ornaments and said, "It's time you started collecting something . . . and I know you like Christmas." Well, that was the beginning of the collecting and decorating that has now become my life's passion and work—and yes, it extended from Christmas to every holiday.

In fact, many of the holiday decorations I use now were ones from that original box from Dad; still others were ones I bought when I was a kid. I am always on the hunt, and my collections have grown by leaps and bounds. As many "new" vintage pieces as I find, I'm still partial to those that belonged to my family (like my grandmother's antique Santa ornament or my nana's trio of choirboy candles). They really do bring comfort, connection, and continuity to my life.

Unwrapping them every year is like seeing old friends. I do, however, use my old things in new ways, and I like to mix up my decorating every year with new themes and displays. As of late, and as you'll see in this book, just about every holiday gets a tree. Trees aren't just for Christmas anymore!

This midcentury card of Santa at his desk is a fun find.

The very first tree I had of my own was decorated for me as a surprise by my brother, Johnny. I still have the ornaments, and I often use them now in different displays. The light-up Santa that was under that tree is the only piece of Christmas I display all year long. When he's not adding joy to one of my holiday vignettes, he's a night-light in my bathroom. Each time I see him is an opportunity to tap into that powerfully happy memory of when Johnny first surprised me with him.

While I decorate a lot for each holiday, I know not everyone does. Sometimes just a pumpkin on the front stoop or a shamrock cutout on the fridge is enough to conjure up those holiday feelings. I also know someone who doesn't decorate a tree any longer, but she puts her mother's ornaments in a crystal bowl on a side table. Every time she passes them, she thinks of her mother.

Like the beloved song "We Need a Little Christmas" implies, when you build it, they will come, and you can include yourself in that group. Contrary to popular belief, I'm not always jolly, or even always in a holiday mood, but once I start decorating, there's a spring in my step—and the rest falls into place.

And when things fall into place, we share memories, and we make memories. That's what holidays are all about in my book. In fact, I'm going to share some with you now. My hope is, as I do this, I can encourage you to do the same. Enjoy *A Very Vintage Holiday*!

—BOB RICHTER

Opposite page: Vintage jigsaw puzzles are perfect for a relaxing holiday afternoon; these are great for the Fourth of July (top). My sister Robin made me this wonderful Christmas card from bits of our grandmother's rickrack (bottom).

This Santa blow mold is the same one my brother Johnny had under my first Christmas tree (page ix). I keep him out all year long as a night-light.

These three puffy ornaments were also on that tree Johnny decorated for me.

Vintage cards are easy to find at flea markets; they make great decorations.

At my house, there's a bouquet or two for every holiday, displayed in vintage pottery.

A bouquet of mums in a vintage jug brings a fresh feel for Halloween decor.

⟡ ┄┄┄┄┄┄┄┄┄┄┄┄┄┄┄┄┄┄┄┄┄┄ ⟡

Vintage plastic cake toppers can be used on a freshly made Halloween treat.

They say penguins mate for life. I bought these vintage blow molds separately on different days at the same flea market from the same dealer. I think they belong together.

Celebrating Holidays
THE VINTAGE WAY

A s America's Vintage Lifestyle Expert, I work to keep the best of the past alive while living and being present today. Sometimes that means making subtle changes to traditions or using vintage objects in new ways (an old family tablecloth becomes a Christmas tree skirt, or old Valentine's cards become decorations for my Valentine's Day tree).

That said, as much as I love the vintage objects I use to decorate and celebrate, the vintage ways are equally important to me. In some cases, they are traditions like hiding Easter eggs or handing out candy to trick-or-treaters. In other instances, they are how we do things, like putting cloves in an orange at Christmas like Mom always did, or saying a special prayer at the Thanksgiving dinner table.

When we use treasured objects, many of which are family heirlooms, and engage in vintage ways, we are keeping love alive. These simple and meaningful acts and moments are how we continue to tell our stories, to bring back memories and make new ones.

In this chapter I'll show a variety of holiday objects and talk about their meaning and how they live on today.

I've tried my best to narrow the holidays down to the ones I celebrate and decorate for the most. Of course there are others, which don't always have as many visuals but are still dear to me. Ever hear of Fastnacht Day? That's the day before Lent (like Fat Tuesday) when Mom would make German doughnuts.

I have such great memories of Mom picking me up at school and bringing me home to make the *fastnachts*. She'd make her own dough and then drop each dollop into a pot of boiling oil. Then she'd let them cool, fill them with her homemade jelly, and top with powdered sugar. That's pretty much it. An opportunity to eat some majorly delicious carbs—and another powerfully happy moment in my life!

These memories all have one thing in common: They represent a time when I slowed down and connected with loved ones. For that reason alone, holidays are wildly important. In fact, I'd go so far as to say that many of these vintage ways are an opportunity to experience *mindfulness*.

Examples include carving pumpkins, dying Easter eggs, and lighting a Christmas tree. When you're doing these things, you can't be texting or scrolling social media. They are opportunities to be present and make memories.

Being present and connecting with family and friends is what holidays are all about, and that's why I love them so much.

Of course, even when we celebrate the same holidays as others, customs and traditions can be different, but the messages of love and connection are still the same.

When I was a kid, I had a giant coloring book called *Christmas Around the World* and I LOVED it. I, of course, colored in it all year long. I have distinct memories of enjoying it over summer vacation. The reason I loved it so much was that it helped me learn about all the different ways people celebrated my favorite holiday in other cultures. For example, in Italy, instead of Santa they have Befana, the good witch who brings gifts; in Norway they decorate special trees for birds and other animals (my family does this too!); and in Australia, since it's summer, they often have picnics at the beach on Christmas Day. I recently found an uncolored vintage copy, so I may just break out my crayons and go to town!

I was raised as a Lutheran, and so when it comes to the holidays of other faiths and cultures, I don't claim to be a great source of knowledge. That said, I do make it my business to know about as many of them as I can. What I've found is that holidays like Passover, Hanukkah, Purim, Diwali, Kwanza, Ramadan, the Lunar New Year, and so many more are all about being present and connecting with family and friends. Most have religious roots, and for that reason they are held in a sacred light, like so many of the holidays I know, love, and celebrate.

My partner is Jewish, so I've had the great privilege of learning about holidays I didn't grow up celebrating. I did, however, go to a great elementary school, where we learned about many of them. I know "The Dreidel Song" by heart, and I learned how to make potato latkes in fourth grade. I was excited to share these tiny connectors to our celebration of Hanukkah as I learned much more about the celebration. Aside from the religious framework and the prayers and songs, I soon realized that the much-loved family menorah at Hanukkah and seder plate at Passover provide the same comfort, connection, and continuity to me that my holiday objects do.

In fact, what holidays show me is that we really are all more alike than we are different. That understanding has the power to break down walls and replace them with windows. I invite you to look through my book and see how much of your family's past and present you can recognize—in both the holidays you celebrated and the holidays you didn't.

My absolute favorite Christmas album of all time is *John Denver and The Muppets: A Christmas Together*. It was one I played over and over as a kid, and I still do to this day. There's so much wisdom and joy and true holiday spirit in that album. It always has me laughing and crying and singing along.

One of my favorite holiday songs on the album is "The Christmas Wish," sung by Kermit the Frog. He explains that it doesn't matter what faith you follow, as long as you believe in love. That's all we need to enjoy this magical time of the year.

It's sung by such a profound frog! It's the way I feel, and I'm so grateful to Kermit for putting it into words for me. So, with that in mind, the common denominators you'll see in every chapter of *A Very Vintage Holiday* are not only how I decorate but also how I celebrate, how I honor my faith, family, and friends with traditions, old and new. My hope is that you'll relate to some of these, and that they'll bring back fond memories of your own.

Mom always made cloved oranges at Christmas, and now I carry on the tradition.

That said, it's very important to me to also honor the traditions and faith of others since, at our very core, we're more alike than different. The Christmas spirit that dwells in my heart is all about peace on Earth and goodwill toward men, women, animals, and all living things. With that in mind, here's what you'll see in the following chapters.

SIX WAYS I MAKE EVERY HOLIDAY A VERY VINTAGE HOLIDAY

1. Carry on a tradition and/or start a new one.

Traditions are at the core of most holidays. They are the things that connect us and continue to imprint memories upon us. Some are very intentional, like dying Easter eggs. Others can be happy accidents, like the Christmas I left the tape recorder I got that year from my grandparents on "record" so it picked up our conversations under the tree. We used that same tape recorder to capture Christmas mornings for decades on audiocassette. I still have those tapes and enjoy listening to them. Today, instead of cassette tapes, everyone gets a little moment captured on video for posterity.

Life goes on, and sometimes traditions must change. If older parents have been the ones to host Thanksgiving, often that baton is passed to the children. Or, as families change, many now celebrate "Friendsgiving" and gather with their adopted family. Even as traditions change and evolve with us, some things can stay the same—for example, your grandmother's stuffing recipe, your grandfather's favorite prayer, or watching the big game together. In these bits that stay the same, we often find that comfort, connection, and continuity. So even if your grandmother or grandfather is no longer on this physical plane, they are very much a part of things. In this way, they live on during some of our happiest most connected times.

2. Use family decorations (or ones like them).

I'm very fortunate to have decorations that belonged to both my maternal and paternal grandmothers. They are among my most cherished holiday items. My paternal grandmother's blown Father Christmas ornament and purple "Silent Night" Shiny Brite ball are very dear to me, and they go on my largest tree every year. Similarly, my nana's choirboy candles are among my most cherished holiday decorations. She always put them on the buffet in the dining room, and now I put them near a favorite photo of her on the sideboard.

Other things were lost or broken, and I've found their counterparts at flea markets and other vintage venues. Just because they didn't actually belong to my family doesn't mean I can't enjoy the memories and feelings they evoke. For example, my mom always had a wonderful ceramic jack-o'-lantern on display every year. Her friend Ellie made it in ceramics class, and we all loved it. At some point it was broken and thrown away. Still, I never forgot that wonderful light-up fellow, and when I saw ones like him at flea markets, I started buying them. Now I have a whole collection. When I see them, I'm transported right back to happy memories of Halloweens past.

If you didn't get special family decorations, go out and find ones like them at flea markets and share the memories they bring back with your loved ones. This is another way the spirit of our family and wonder of our childhood can be with us at these very special times.

3. Make, bake, or mail something.

I grew up in a very crafty family, so handmade gifts are my personal favorites. As a kid I was encouraged to make gifts and cards and was taught how to do everything from embroidery to quilling to decoupage. There's an awful lot of heart in a homemade gift, and I cherish the ones I'm given. I am fortunate to still have crafty and artistic friends, so whether these items are cards or ornaments, hats or scarves, I love them all. Every year Mom knits me something, my sister sews me something, and my dear friend Sharon draws me something. To me, these are some of the loveliest gifts of all.

As a kid, I made holiday ornaments and strung popcorn and cranberries for the Christmas tree. When I do those things now, the memories come

back, and the good feelings start to bubble up. I strung popcorn and cranberries this year for a tree in my dining room, and it made me think of so many happy times doing the same thing back in my childhood.

Jack-o-lantern carving is a fun, mindful Halloween activity.

© Getty Images/E+/Adam Smigielski

The same goes for baking. Every year Mom and my sister Robin bake. And bake and bake and bake. I get about thirteen different kinds of cookies, and in addition to enjoying the way they taste, I have come to realize that baking and cooking really are expressions of love. The same goes for those handmade items. Consider a handmade gift or home-baked item this year. It is a magnificent way to show someone they are loved!

Also under this category would be sending physical greeting cards. A "Happy Birthday" text just isn't the same as an actual written card sent in the mail. I'm a sentimental saver; I have cards from all holidays past, and they are wonderful to enjoy on a cold evening. In fact, often weeks *after* Christmas, I reread all my holiday cards before putting them away. It's a nice way to wrap up the season.

4. Give your time and be present.

Time is the most precious gift of all. We're all busy—especially so at the holidays—so I have come to greatly appreciate when someone gives me their time. Perhaps it's to watch a movie, share a cup of hot cocoa, or just enjoy a long, overdue phone call.

This could even be attending church services or going shopping or wrapping gifts together. Other joyful, connected moments might include going to see a holiday concert or a play or sporting event. Any way you slice it, the gift of time is often the piece of the giving pie that means the most and makes people happiest.

Giving your time doesn't have to include just your friends and family. Some of my most beloved holiday memories are ones where I volunteered to help others. I find these opportunities most rewarding, and they make me feel more connected to my community. They could include playing Santa for a family in need or visiting those who don't have any biological family.

5. Share a meal.

Whether it is around the kitchen table, on a picnic blanket, or in a restaurant, dining together is a key ingredient in celebrating holidays the vintage way. In a world where many families don't all gather 'round the dining table together each night, holidays help us stop and be intentional about sharing a meal (or two or three or five) together.

Make it extra special by having flowers and candles and using your good china. These touches make even the most ordinary meal special and memorable.

While you're all around the table, why not ask each person to share something they are grateful for (we do this at Thanksgiving), proud of (we do this at Passover), or intent on manifesting (we do this on New Year's Eve).

6. Do something interactive.

At some point during every holiday, usually later in the day after opening presents or the big meal, my family plays a game. Whether it's *Trivial Pursuit*, *Skip-Bo*, or *Taboo*, we connect and laugh and make memories. The same goes for jigsaw puzzles. They are very vintage and help create a common goal and lots of time to talk and connect.

My family is very big on classic Hollywood films. Since most holidays have some films devoted to them, we usually watch favorite ones and laugh, cry, and sing along at the same parts every year. I'll list some of my favorites in the following chapters.

Singing is also a great way to connect. Whether it's a sing-along of holiday carols or a karaoke

birthday party (yes, I've had more than one of those!), people loosen up, have fun, laugh, and create memories that bring us all closer together. And don't forget about singing in the car (I always did with Mom), singing in church (I was in the choir and loved every minute of it), and yes, singing while decorating the tree ("The 12 Days of Christmas" is a good one for that!).

Stringing popcorn and cranberries takes me right back to childhood.

A common denominator of these six categories is *mindfulness*. With the holidays typically being a very busy time, these activities can help us slow down and connect. What a gift that is, in and of itself! Here's the real challenge: Try your best to put down your phone and just be present in all the above. You'll be amazed at just how wonderful it all is when you're not worried about posting a picture to social media the very moment it's happening. Take the photos, certainly—but post them later!

In each of the following chapters, I'll share my experience and ideas about how to tap into these vintage ways and make every holiday *A Very Vintage Holiday*.

BOB'S RULES FOR A VERY VINTAGE HOLIDAY DECORATING

Many people have told me they are inspired by the way I decorate and have taken some of my ideas and made them their own. This of course makes me very happy; it's the greatest compliment ever!

Here are the rules:

1. There *are* no rules.
2. Don't worry about what other people think. Decorate for yourself and your family.
3. Have fun!

Now that I've gotten that off my chest, here are some *guidelines* for how I decorate. You'll see these play out in the photographs in this book. Since they are only guidelines, think of them like items on a salad bar: Take what you like and leave the rest!

BOB'S SIX VERY VINTAGE HOLIDAY DECORATING TIPS

1. Let color and symmetry be your guides.

My living room has a lot of blue and cream, so it's a nice basic palette. When I add black and orange, it starts to look and feel like Halloween. As much as I add decorations with these colors (jack-o'-lanterns, etc.), I also bring items from other rooms, such as vases, that are orange and black. I try to balance the colors in all the spaces, and by the time I'm done, the room is transformed.

I grew up in the family business, which was interior design, upholstery, window treatments, etc. There Nana trained me to use color to tell the story. She also taught me an appreciation for balance, which becomes very important when you have a lot of decorations like I do. Symmetry helps bring harmony. Sometimes I get wacky and do an asymmetrical display, like my kitchen island of jack-o'-lantern blow molds for Halloween, but I still rely on color to make it cohesive.

2. Go for a feeling and a look rather than a period.

My Independence Day decorations hail from many eras, but the red, white, and blue unite them, and the feelings they evoke when I put them all together are joyful, patriotic, and celebratory.

3. Embrace modern technology and new items to make things easier and safer.

While I love all things vintage, I really do enjoy living today. I take advantage of items like LED tea lights with built-in timers and new artificial pre-lit trees. They make less work for me and help me enjoy the fun parts of decorating.

This Christmas I used those LED lights inside antique fairy lamps on a tree in my dining room. Originally these lamps used real candles and thus were not the safest

or easiest choice for holiday decorating. I get the same look with less worry and fuss, and I am grateful we live in a time where these choices are so readily available. And while I love the look of vintage tree lights, in addition to safety concerns, when they burn out, the whole string goes out. I happily use mostly new lights and spend a lot less time changing bulbs. More time for me to enjoy my decorations rather than trying to keep them lit!

4. Use old things in new ways.

I use Nana's bird clothespins as Christmas tree decorations and one of Mom's Christmas earrings as a lapel pin. I use mixing bowls as tree stands and sugar bowls to hold candy. If something has sentimental value, use it! Just because something belonged to your grandmother doesn't mean you have to use it the same way she did.

Mom's Christmas earrings and pin add a festive, sentimental touch to my lapel and cap at the holidays.

I also love color-blocking with everyday objects to add a holiday feel (red and white pottery for Valentine's Day; orange and black glassware for Halloween). Even though these objects on their own have nothing to do with the holiday, when grouped together, they make a very festive impact.

Since there are no rules, consider using decorations made for a specific purpose in a new way. My latest favorite examples of this? For St. Patrick's Day I used one of those crepe paper table centerpieces as a tree topper, and it looked amazing! For Halloween I used an old paper cat cutout meant to put on the wall in the center of a pumpkin wreath; it created a one-of-a-kind piece that was so easy to do and brought me tons of joy.

5. Add something fresh or natural.

Plants, cut flowers, or branches of the season literally add life to your decorating. They invigorate everything and add a very inviting energy—sometimes even a lovely fragrance.

I try to bring cuttings in from my yard and local farms for every holiday. I have many live Christmas trees, and the smell is magical. I typically leave the tree undecorated for a while, just so I can enjoy its majesty. This taps into the activities around the winter solstice, where bringing greens inside was part of the ritual to honor the change in seasons.

Adding bits of nature is a great way to bring a greater dimension and even a metaphor to your decorating. So every Easter I have hyacinths and tulips, and every Thanksgiving I have pressed leaves and bittersweet. It is very vintage and very comforting.

6. Add fun, decorative things in unexpected places.

Mom always put a rubber pixie on the wall phone in our kitchen, and it made me so happy. I have holiday decor all over my home, and the kitchen and bathroom are included in the fun.

A friend once told me I inspired her to put a Christmas tree in her bathroom. She was worried people would think she was odd, but when she saw that I did it, she followed suit; it became her favorite tree of all that year. Per my "rules" above, don't worry about what people think. Decorate in ways and in places that make you happy. We spend a lot of time in the bathroom, so it seems the perfect place for holiday decor!

This year for Halloween, I put a vintage store display hand in an old box near all the candy. I added a few LED tea lights, and it was the star of my decorating vignettes. Let your imagination take the lead, and have fun!

In addition to my decorated spaces, in each chapter I'll showcase some favorite items from my collection and talk a little bit about what makes them special.

Now that I've shared my tips for vintage ways and decorating, without further ado, let's get onto the holidays! I've decided to let the calendar be my guide, so chapter 2 will kick off a full year's worth of holiday celebrations. Drum roll, please. . . . Let the decorating and celebrating begin! Here comes A Very Vintage Holiday!

My partner's family Haggadah was passed down by his great-grandmother and is still used at Passover.

Bob's Must-Have Helpers for A Very Vintage Holiday

My displays rely largely on my imagination and the tips I've shared in this chapter, but I also need a few practical things to help bring my visions of sugar plums, jack-o'-lanterns, shamrocks, and more come to life. These are a few of the essentials:

- **Fishing line.** Since it is both strong and invisible, fishing line can make objects appear to be floating, flying, etc.
- **Wax adhesive.** Meant for keeping candles straight in their holders, I use this for a myriad of things to keep them straight or secure.
- **Vintage cans and canisters.** I use these to raise objects and vary heights in my displays.
- **Twist ties.** I use these to fasten lights, hold tree toppers in place, etc.
- **Thumbtacks.** Most of the vintage cardboard cutouts I use have a small hole in the top meant for a string. I use that hole for a tack to hang each one rather than putting tape on the back, which can cause damage.
- **Power strips.** I plug in a lot of things, and power strips make it easy to turn many items on and off with one touch.
- **LED tea lights.** I have mentioned these. They are wonderful, and I use them everywhere. The better ones have a built-in timer, which is a real time-saver.

- **Sturdy ladder.** I do a lot of climbing, so I need a very good ladder. A big thanks to my sister Robin for getting me an excellent one!
- **Packing tape.** I often roll a piece of packing tape into a ball to level something or keep it in place.
- **Paper clips.** They hold 3-D paper decorations in place and can act as a makeshift hook for hanging just about anything.

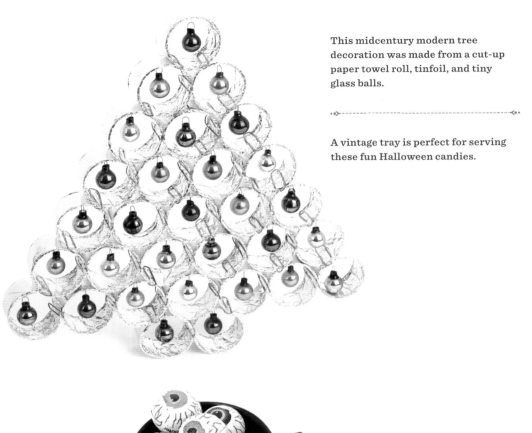

This midcentury modern tree decoration was made from a cut-up paper towel roll, tinfoil, and tiny glass balls.

A vintage tray is perfect for serving these fun Halloween candies.

My talented friend Sharon made me this lovely holiday decoration, which has become an instant heirloom in my home.

•❧• - •❧•

Two vintage heart-shaped doilies glued together make a charming card or decoration. The box was a gift from my friend Amy, who adorned it with vintage cutouts.

Mom had this same pair of ceramic pilgrims in slightly different colors. I found this set at a flea market, and they add a sentimental touch to my holiday decor.

I love using old things in new ways. This large blow mold jack-o-lantern was made for trick-or-treating. Now I use it as a planter for the season.

I once attended a Christmas celebration at a family's home where they had this large figure of Baby Jesus on the table. After dinner, we all gathered around the table and sang "Happy Birthday" to him. I thought it was such a sweet thing.

Vintage cookie cutters with a bit of ribbon tied to them make great decorations—especially for a kitchen Christmas tree.

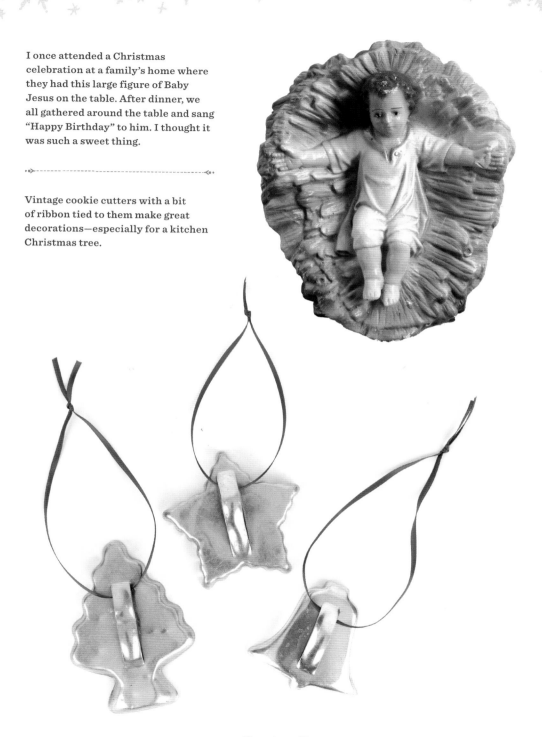

New Year's Eve

EPIPHANY

New Year's is a much-anticipated time of celebration, and with Christmas decorations still in place, it is especially festive. Many celebrate for the whole week between Christmas and New Year's Day, and often that celebrating culminates on December 31.

Noisemakers, horns, and party hats are commonly associated with this holiday. I collect the vintage versions and use them each year, not only for their intended purpose but also as decorations. Streamers, paper banners, and images of Father Time and Baby New Year are also a nostalgic nod to this joyful time.

Of course it's a time for parties, resolutions, and new beginnings. For many, it's also the culmination of a week of merriment. Many wonderful vintage images portray Father Time signing off and Baby New Year signing in.

For me New Year's Eve is about both reflecting back and looking forward. I don't like to use the word "resolution," but I do make goals. While many crowd into Times Square or gather for big parties, I enjoy a quieter evening of contemplation and goal setting.

New Year's Day is also a holiday where people typically gather for a big meal and togetherness. Traditional food runs the gamut from pork and sauerkraut to black-eyed peas.

The
WESTERN
HORSEMAN
JANUARY 1964 • 50 CENTS

HAPPY NEW YEAR!

SIX WAYS I CELEBRATE A VERY VINTAGE NEW YEAR

1. Carry on a tradition and/or start a new one.

When I was a kid, Mom would make New Year's Eve special by making a picnic for us on the living room floor. One year we came home and my sister Robin had stocked the fridge with shrimp cocktail and all sorts of goodies. We ate and watched a good old movie musical like *South Pacific* or *Oklahoma!,* and of course we sang along with the singing parts.

Since then, I have had New Year's Eves with fancy parties and exotic locations, but now I'm back to wanting to be at home with my partner doing what my mom had planned all those years ago. We do basically the same thing as I did when I was a kid, except we cook together and try a new recipe every year, often from a new cookbook one of us received for Christmas.

On New Year's Day, Mom would make pork and sauerkraut and all the family would come for a meal. We'd eat and laugh and share our resolutions. Now my partner and I typically have leftovers from what we cooked on New Year's Eve and share what we feel were accomplishments from the old year and our intentions for the new.

2. Use family decorations (or ones like them).

Since Christmas decorations are still in full swing at my house, I've started creating a tree that's just for New Year's. It's silver, and I decorated it with vintage foil stars like ones I made when I was a kid. Underneath are hats and horns like ones I wore and used. At midnight, we use them—the rest of the time they stay there, looking fun and festive as holiday decor.

3. Make, bake, or mail something.

Each year my partner makes a family calendar with photos from happy moments of everyone over the past year. Each family member gets a copy, and it is a lovely way to say "I love you" to all and start the year off in a very sweet way. Putting up the new calendar then becomes a tradition on January 1 and feels like a nice way to memorialize New Year's.

Also, this is a time when I often write thank-you cards. I typically do this on New Year's Day while all the holiday decor is still around me and the opened gifts are nearby under the trees. I find my heart is very full of gratitude, and this is a wonderful moment to share it.

4. Give your time and be present.

Every New Year's Eve, I call my family at midnight and wish them a Happy New Year. On New Year's Day I call and catch up with my best friends and often one friend I feel I've been missing and haven't talked with in a long while. Sometimes these have even been old teachers of mine. It's a lovely way to start the year—feeling grounded and connected and sharing love with those you love.

5. Share a meal.

I've already mentioned cooking a new meal every year, but here I'll mention the setting. We eat all our meals at the dining room table. Like all the furniture in the dining room, it belonged to my grandparents, and it has a great deal of emotional value to me.

Around the table on New Year's Day is where we share those accomplishments and goals I mentioned earlier. For my own personal growth, I've found it's very powerful to share these things with those you love and trust. It often becomes a catalyst for conversation and a way to feel like you're tying up the old year and stepping lively into the new one.

Hurrah for the Heather,
Each sprig that we pluck,
Contains a sweet message
and brings you Good Luck.

HAPPY 365 DAYS

6. Do something interactive.

I've already mentioned that we stay home on New Year's Eve, and when we do, *Scrabble* is the game we enjoy playing. I have lots of memories of playing it with my family growing up, and my partner has taught me how to really strategize, make multiple words at once, and be a bit of a boss when it comes to this old-fashioned game. That said, we help each other win and have often tied or had games where the scores were nearly the same in the end. It's a nice way to be, and I'm grateful to start the year with someone who is rooting for me and vice versa. Typically, by the time we're done with dinner and the game, it's midnight and "Happy New Year" time.

A VERY VINTAGE NEW YEAR'S DECORATING

As I mentioned, my New Year's decor is simple and, of course, vintage. The silver tree decorated with stars feels like a nod to the future; the vintage horns and hats underneath are both nostalgic and celebratory.

To play out the metaphor of past and future, I used a new pre-lit silver tree, but the stars are vintage. They are likely from a department store or church, because I found one hundred of them (enough to decorate an enormous tree). I also liked the idea that they looked like the kind of stars I made as a kid by cutting

out the star shape from cardboard and wrapping each one in aluminum foil. They are fun and joyful and celebratory, which feels just right for New Year's. I topped it all off with a wonderful vintage silver angel holding a wand with a star on the end of it.

I like the lines of the new tree, which really enable you to see the stars. It's also a lot easier to put up than those vintage silver trees where each branch has to be put into one of the many holes in the wooden pole. I've often found a few of the holes are chipped, and a branch or two doesn't fit as it should. So I skipped the hassle, streamlined the process, and went for a more contemporary feel.

To add extra pizzazz and a very vintage vibe, I used a 1960s color wheel that was the regular companion to those vintage silver trees. The reflection of each of the four colors on the tree, the stars—even the room in general—is downright magical. This becomes the WOW factor and is relatively easy to achieve. Vintage color wheels are readily available at flea markets, and many retailers are producing new ones. As with anything electric, there are instances where I recommend buying new to avoid safety or functionality concerns.

That's how I played out the metaphors of New Year's Eve in my decor: the best of the past, a joyful present, and a future reaching for the stars.

On my table I include fresh flowers, candles, and vintage china. That combination could describe my table on pretty much any day of the year, but I love using fresh, new (in the world of vintage that typically means "new to me") items to add to the symbolism of the New Year.

A vintage color wheel magically transforms this tree and brings fun and nostalgia to this corner of my home.

Epiphany

For many cultures the Epiphany is an even bigger day of celebration than Christmas Day. January 6 is recognized as the day when the Three Wise Men (also called the Magi) brought their gifts to the Christ Child. Thus, in honor of those gift bearers, Epiphany is a day of giving. In Spain, for example, this is the day when all gifts are exchanged; and in many Eastern European countries, it is referred to as "Little Christmas."

When I was a kid, Theresa, a family friend, celebrated Little Christmas. When we visited her to celebrate, gifts were exchanged, carols were played, and decorations were vibrantly displayed. In short, the Christmas train had *not* left the station like it does for many after January 1.

As it turns out, December 25 is really the *first* day of Christmas. Everyone knows "The Twelve Days of Christmas" (my favorite version is by John Denver and The Muppets), and those dozen days are really about celebrating, as the song connotes. So the twelfth day of Christmas is January 6, and that day deserves its own celebration.

While I don't engage in all my *Six Ways* for this holiday, I often give little gifts to those I love, sing "The Twelve Days of Christmas," and wrap up my holiday celebrating for the season.

It feels like a gift to have this extra time in a world where we're typically told Christmas is over six days earlier. I always think of our friend Teresa with gratitude and enjoy my decorations to the fullest, as she did.

To conclude my celebrations, I often watch the classic film *O. Henry's Full House*. It features several of O. Henry's most popular stories, culminating with "The Gift of The Magi." The story, beautifully told in this film, showcases the pure love of a couple who give each other the most meaningful gifts in spite of their financial challenges. I won't give away the story if you don't yet know it, but it is a real tearjerker. Happy tears, of course! The best kind!

A VERY VINTAGE EPIPHANY DECORATING

Since all my holiday decor is still up and in all its glory, I often showcase my collections of Three Wise Men figures, candleholders, and decorations in front of my trees and other displays.

It's more of a refreshing than a decorating, as I gather all the wise men figures and give them center stage. I light the candles, sing "We Three Kings" and other carols, give a few small, heartfelt gifts, and make merry.

A vintage party hat is great to wear or just use as a decoration.

It's hard to find vintage New Year's decorations, so I was excited when I came across this cute ceramic gal sporting a Happy New Year sash.

These fun vintage horns and noisemakers have great colors and graphics.

This horn and noisemaker are among the oldest in my collection, hailing from the 1930s–40s.

A vintage party napkin featuring Baby New Year.

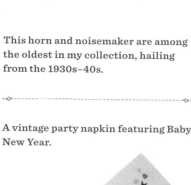

Another suite of noisemakers from the 1950s–60s. They have such fun images on them.

I found this 1960s set of Wise Men candle holders in their original box. They make a great Epiphany display.

The wild colors of these Three Wise Men figures are evocative of the late 1960s. Made of papier-mâché and hand-painted, they are a lot of fun.

The Three Kings, as produced by Playmobil. I love their colors and details and enjoy displaying them in my kitchen.

•❯------------------------------------❮•

This tiny trio of The Magi is German and hand-painted.

•❯------------------------------------❮•

A midcentury holiday card featuring three crowns for the Three Kings.

Valentine's Day

February 14 is the day we celebrate love. While historically a day to celebrate romantic love, it has evolved into a much more inclusive day to honor all kinds of love.

Remember decorating a shoebox to collect the valentines you received in school? I sure do. And of course, what a big deal it was to pick out the pack of valentines you'd give to your classmates each year.

Speaking of cards, how about the homemade ones? As far as I'm concerned, nothing beats a homemade valentine card. I love the ones that use heart-shaped paper doilies and construction paper. As much as these are associated with kids, I think it's extra special when adults exchange them. My partner makes one for me every year, and it's my favorite card of all.

Did you know that the first valentine is reported to have been sent in the fifteenth century? It wasn't until the mid-nineteenth century, however, that Valentine's Day cards really took off. They were typically postcards and remained that way until well after the turn of the century, when they became more elaborate—some even were made like pop-up cards.

Flowers and candy are also very central to Valentine's Day gifting and celebrating. Heart-shaped boxes filled with chocolates, Sweethearts candies with cute messages printed on them, red roses, and pink carnations are all traditional offerings at this time of year. Those heart-shaped boxes date back to the 1860s, and the tradition of giving flowers dates all the way back to the seventeenth century.

Cupid, of course, is a figure from Roman mythology, while Saint Valentine is reported to have been a Roman priest in the third century. The history around this holiday goes on and on—and like many holidays, it has its roots in paganism and even a fertility festival that happened around February 14. Another theory about the reason we celebrate Valentine's Day on February 14 is because that's when birds start mating. Listen to Cole Porter's "Let's Do It, Let's Fall in Love" sometime! It's all in there!

No matter what piece of history is true or honored, what really matters is that this is a day of love—all kinds of love. Share it!

SIX WAYS I CELEBRATE A VERY VINTAGE VALENTINE'S DAY

1. Carry on a tradition and/or start a new one.

Every year on Valentine's Day, I send flowers to those I love (my partner, my mom, etc.). It's something I've always done on some level. Even as a kid, I'd give Mom a rose or something to symbolize the love in my heart for her. Now, in addition to those in my inner circle, I also choose someone who might really need a lift and send them flowers as well. Sometimes it's a person who has just had a loss or is facing some sort of challenge.

Opening my heart and sharing it with others is what Valentine's Day is all about, and this tradition is one I love. If I can make someone's day, my heart just gets even fuller.

2. Use family decorations (or ones like them).

My mom always had those red cupid cutouts on the kitchen wall every year on Valentine's Day. They were also in my classrooms at school. Since they are such a part of my personal history, I like using them today. In addition to putting them on my kitchen wall, I also put them in the windows.

3. Make, bake, or mail something.

I love sending vintage valentines to everyone on my list. I typically find the ones we used to send in school at flea markets and other vintage venues. They are often very "punny" and sweet, and typically they are used. Instead of crossing out the name on the old valentine, I just add "and Bob" after it. So, if it says "Love, Clara," I change it to read "Love, Clara & Bob." After all, it was originally from Clara! This little touch makes people smile and often remember those simpler days of classroom valentine exchanges.

Some years I have also made my own valentines—done in the vintage way, of course. All you need is some red construction paper, wrapping paper, and doilies. I remember making them as a kid. You fold the construction paper in half, draw a half heart, cut it out, and then open it to reveal a nice, big heart. I sometimes do the same with vintage wrapping paper and doilies. I have made them in graduated sizes and then glued one on top of the other to create a very vintage-looking valentine!

4. Give your time and be present.

Since Valentine's Day is about celebrating love, I like to visit those I love and deliver a sweet, a card, and a little gift. For older loved ones, I often ask them about their favorite Valentine's Day memory. Often I'll learn something I never knew about that person and enjoy not only a bit of their history but also a snapshot of the world before my time in it.

5. Share a meal.

As I mentioned, my partner and I have dinner at the dining room table every night, but on Valentine's Day we typically enjoy a longer meal while we exchange gifts (usually a photo of the two of us from sometime during the past year). Of course we present them to each other in vintage frames!

6. Do something interactive.

Since Valentine's Day often falls on a weeknight, there isn't a ton of time to do things other than share a meal and gifts, but one fun activity we've added to the mix is reading an old love card, letter, or email to each other from years past. As I've mentioned, I'm a sentimental saver, so uncovering one of these items is easy. Often we'll also look at photos from a special vacation or day and laugh and reminisce. That's my idea of a fun evening!

A VERY VINTAGE VALENTINE'S DAY DECORATING

Since I've barely taken down all the Christmas/New Year's/Epiphany decorations by the time Valentine's Day rolls around, I concentrate my decorating to the kitchen and the dining room. While red and pink are the predominant colors, I change up the mood for each room. The kitchen is more playful, and the dining room is more romantic.

In the kitchen, I decorated with those cardboard cutouts like Mom used to use. I arranged them around the tree and even fashioned one into a tree topper. For ornaments, I used those old valentine cards like we used to give out in school. I tucked them into the branches of the tree, and they give off a vibe that's both sweet and sentimental. I added cupids and angel Christmas ornaments that look wonderful and are very fitting for a Valentine's Day tree.

Under the tree, there are more angels, as well as elves and pixies to add to the joyful vibe. Of course I peppered in cut flowers in small vintage vases. I also used some great red and white–striped kitchen canisters. Since it is the kitchen, I couldn't help but add a box of vintage dish detergent because the font and colors were so wonderful. It's hard not to smile when you see this display.

In the dining room, I saved time by using the same tree that was up at Christmas. Once I removed all those icicles and other decorations, I was left with softly lit branches, to which I added vintage blown-glass ornaments in various heart shapes. I also added some wonderful 1950s German wax cupid ornaments. Although these are Christmas ornaments, they are all hearts and cupids, so the look is decidedly Valentine's Day.

For a finishing touch, I strung bits of vintage rickrack around the tree. I love old trim, as it reminds me of things my family would use when crafting or in our family business. On either side of the tree, I arranged some vintage red pottery and candy boxes to add harmony.

Fun and romance are on the menu for Valentine's Day, so why not drive the point home with my vintage decor?

I love a handmade Valentine's Day card. These two vintage kits helped kids make them.

Vintage cupid silhouettes like this one bring back lots of memories. They came in all sizes, and I use them to decorate walls, trees, packages, and more.

Vintage valentine cardboard wall decorations like these are easily found in just about every vintage venue. I pick them up all year long and use them to decorate, and often gift them as well.

A heart-shaped paper doily like this one adds a nice touch to a plate of sweet treats. I also use them to make my own Valentine's Day cards.

Vintage Valentine cards are fun to collect and gift. I especially like the fancy ones with added honeycomb elements.

"GOBS" OF LOVE

TO MY Valentine!

Made in U.S.A.

Small valentine cards like these
were typically given to students and
teachers alike. I like to use them to
decorate my Valentine's Day trees.

This vintage heart-shaped ring box
would be a great way to package a piece
of jewelry gifted for Valentine's Day.

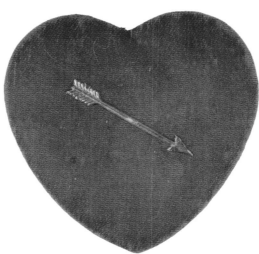

Known for their humorous puns, these vintage Valentine's Day cards are easily found in vintage venues and fun to collect and gift.

Because of their nostalgic graphics and cute puns, I love using vintage valentines like these to decorate my Valentine's Day trees.

To My Valentine
MASKING you to be mine

I'M SPENDIN' MY TIME LOVIN' YE,

very fair
happy days
nice times
stormy gloomy weather showers

Love makes the weather
When we are together!

IT'S TIME -

The variety of vintage valentines you can find out there at flea markets is amazing. Some even have little 3D honeycomb touches.

4 U

PLANE AS ABC

A vintage vase is a great way to gift flowers to your valentine. I keep an eye out for them all year long. I also use carafes and candy holders to gift and display flowers.

Since love is at the heart of Valentine's Day, why not find a vintage card to tell your sweetheart how you feel?

Presidents' Day

When I was a kid, these incredible cherry candies were given out to celebrate George Washington's birthday. The cherry part was pure sugar I suppose—kind of like a lollipop—and they were connected to a green plastic stem. Of course they were underscoring the famous story about young George chopping down the cherry tree and then telling his father about it with that famous line: "I cannot tell a lie."

Over the years I've found some very cool ephemera around that same story, such as axes that were candy containers, gummed stickers, and more. I have collected them all and use them to decorate.

I've also learned that the story of Washington's honesty about the cherry tree was allegedly made up by his publicity person of the day. Oh well, it is part of our popular culture now, so true or false, it's very much associated with George Washington.

For Abe Lincoln, there are many children's books about his young life and rise to the presidency. I remember reading them as a kid and loving them. He was, and still is, very much a role model for kids who want to "grow up and be president" someday.

Like Washington, Lincoln was praised for his honesty. "Honest Abe" was a nickname he was given that stuck, and he was reportedly just fine with it.

Presidents' Day started with only George Washington in 1879. Lincoln was added to the mix in 1970. Die-cut cardboard decorations of both presidents, along with other patriotic ephemera, were often used to decorate classrooms, etc.

SIX WAYS I CELEBRATE A VERY VINTAGE PRESIDENTS' DAY

1. Carry on a tradition and/or start a new one.

As a kid, I thought Presidents' Day was a really big deal because we got the day off from school. Before the holiday, however, we always made cardboard cutout decorations and got to eat those cherry candies I talked about. Now, each year I buy myself some and share them with friends and family.

2. Use family decorations (or ones like them).

I have found some great ephemera for Presidents' Day, much of which was made by kids in school (paper and paint-by-number profiles of each president), and more. I decorate with them and remember how I made ones like them when I was a kid.

3. Make, bake, or mail something.

Every year on Presidents' Day, Mom made a cherry pie or a cherry custard. Now, since I have her recipes, I get to do it. These simple homemade goodies are very tasty as well as very vintage.

4. Give your time and be present.

Since many people have off from work for this holiday, I always think it's nice to get together and go for a hike (weather permitting) or just have a nice old-fashioned visit. It's also a great time to share gratitude for our forefathers and how they laid the foundation for our freedom.

5. Share a meal.

After dinner, it's that cherry custard or cherry pie for dessert. Often, it's also a time to reminisce about childhood memories of this holiday and compare notes on how we celebrated. Because holidays unite us, sharing these memories always makes for fun dinner table conversation.

6. Do something interactive.

There are so many great biopic movies about both presidents, but I enjoy watching a movie with family and friends: *George Washington Slept Here*, with Jack Benny and Ann Sheridan. Although in no way about the father of our country, it is about the mystique of owning a historic property where George Washington may have actually slept. Since I live a hop, skip, and jump from where Washington crossed the Delaware (and where this movie takes place), it is a real treat.

Another fun activity idea in honor of the "honesty" component/propaganda we heard as kids is to play "Two Truths and a Lie." You share three things about yourself, one of which is *not* true, and the other players have to guess which one is the lie.

A VERY VINTAGE PRESIDENTS' DAY DECORATING

This year I made a Presidents' Day tree from some branches I bent and arranged in a wonderful, whimsical anthropomorphic pottery tree vase I found in an antiques shop in Upstate New York. I decorated it with those candy cherries, and the result was super cute.

On either side of it, I placed a vintage paint-by-number portrait of each president. I then added vintage papier-mâché candy containers in the shape of axes, decorated with cherries and George Washington decals. They are so wonderful and so beautifully made; it just goes to show that people took this holiday (and that cherry tree metaphor) very seriously!

I created the whole display in front of a framed map of the USA I found at a local thrift store. Made by National Geographic in the 1950s, it provides a literal backdrop of our country to honor our Founding Fathers.

Since Presidents' Day is so close to Valentine's Day, I don't do more decorating than this, but it is enough to conjure up a bit of nostalgia for my childhood and share some of those memories with loved ones.

To add to the fun, we eat the candy that's hanging on the tree!

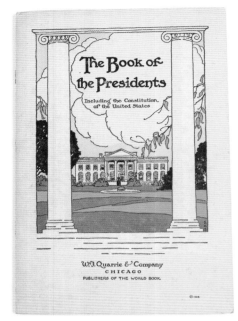

This little vintage paper book I found at a flea market has great historical value and fun graphics.

⬥- -⬥

These rare patriotic candy containers were clearly made to celebrate Washington's birthday. The axe heads come off, and the body can be filled with sweet treats. I use them as part of my Presidents' Day display.

These cardboard decorations of
Washington and Lincoln were in every
classroom I had from kindergarten
to elementary school. I found a pair
at my local flea market and love the
nostalgic vibe they have for me.

Some kid long ago made this
decoration to celebrate Washington's
birthday, and some parent saved
it. Now it's a favorite piece in my
collection.

St. Patrick's Day

They say that everyone's Irish on St. Patrick's Day. While the day's beginnings were rooted in religion, it has evolved into a celebration of a culture. I love how it has been embraced by everyone, no matter their heritage or genealogy.

As a kid, I remember wearing green to school on that day and often being treated to a Shamrock Shake at McDonald's. Irish soda bread and corned beef and cabbage were standard fare for dinner. There was always a St. Patrick's Day parade with lots of merriment and lots and lots of green clothing and accessories.

Decorations included leprechauns, pots of gold, and much more. I've collected many of these items and use them to decorate a St. Patrick's Day tree in my kitchen. Shiny cardboard shamrock cutouts were omnipresent in my childhood classrooms and at home, so I love using them now.

SIX WAYS I CELEBRATE A VERY VINTAGE ST. PATRICK'S DAY

1. Carry on a tradition and/or start a new one.

It's the day for wearing green! As a kid, I always wore a green outfit on Saint Patrick's Day and loved the solidarity it created with fellow students and teachers alike. As an adult, I modify the green choices a bit, but you can usually find me in a green sweater and green socks, at the very least. And I still enjoy that feeling that I'm part of a celebration just by opting in on a color that's already a favorite of mine!

2. Use family decorations (or ones like them).

Like many of the other holidays, I really enjoy using the cardboard cutouts I remember for home and school. They are typically shamrocks, leprechauns, and pots of gold—and the primary color, of course, is green. I've found plenty at flea markets that are just like the ones from my youth.

3. Make, bake, or mail something.

Since spring is on the way, I like giving potted plants as gifts at this time of the year. To drive home the lucky Saint Patrick's Day metaphor, I go for either green oxalis or money plants. I like to put each one in a vintage green planter as part of the overall gift.

For Saint Patrick's Day cards, I try to use vintage ones; it's also fun to add a lottery ticket inside each of them!

4. Give your time and be present.

St. Patrick's Day is a fun holiday to celebrate good luck and fortune, and I think it's a great time to share your good fortune with others. I am a huge fan of random acts of kindness, where you do something nice and don't tell anyone about it. One example would be to put a little cash or a pre-paid credit card in a St. Patrick's Day card and slide it under the door of someone who could really use it. As a note, you can say, "It's a lucky day, so here's a little something to let you know more good luck is on the way!"

5. Share a meal.

While corned beef and cabbage is not my favorite meal, I do like channeling the St. Patrick's Day spirit at the dinner table. So instead I serve green foods like pesto chicken and green beans, with mint ice cream for dessert. Serving all of it on white or even green china is really smile-inducing and makes the point while I serve foods I enjoy!

6. Do something interactive.

A town close to where I live has a huge bingo night on St. Patrick's Day (tapping into the lucky vibe of the day), serves a nice dinner, and even has live entertainment. In other years, I've had a game night at home playing *Monopoly*. It's a fun way to come together and commemorate this historically lucky day!

A VERY VINTAGE ST. PATRICK'S DAY DECORATING

After the red of Valentine's Day comes the green of St. Patrick's Day. And so my kitchen goes from warm to cool as color tells the story.

This year, once again, I used those great vintage cardboard decorations on the wall, around a small pre-lit tree, to which I added shamrock party lights from the 1980s. I decked the tree with smaller versions of those cardboard cutouts and felt leprechauns from the 1960s. My friend Renee also made me some incredible leprechauns from vintage paper scraps and bits of green chenille pipe cleaners. They have such great personality! On top I used a honeycomb top hat table decoration with even more leprechauns busy at work decorating with shamrocks.

Under the tree, I have one of my favorite decorations—a vintage Hallmark redheaded pixie jumping out of a green honeycomb top hat. She is pure joy. On either side I color-blocked green and yellow vintage kitchen items and peppered in some pixies and other fanciful ceramic pieces I've found at flea markets. Like all my displays, I topped it all off with some fresh-cut flowers. It feels very happy-go-lucky!

This hand-painted ceramic St. Patrick's Day lass has loads of charm.

· ❖ ·‑‑‑ ❖ ·

Mom had this cardboard decoration of an Irish fellow doing the jig. I now use him every year when I decorate.

They say everyone's Irish on St. Patrick's Day. This vintage button has the same sentiment.

This vintage leprechaun cardboard house decoration is super cute.

I love these vintage 3D honeycomb displays. I find they also make great toppers for St. Patrick's Day trees.

The humble doily is a classic piece of vintage St. Patrick's Day decor.

This tiny magazine was ideal for the 1950s woman to pop in her purse. I love the cover of this St. Patrick's Day issue.

I found this shamrock planter at a flea market and added a money plant. I think it makes a great gift for St. Patrick's Day.

These joyful 1960s cardboard cutout wall decorations make it easy to add a touch of vintage to any space.

Vintage seals for every holiday! I remember my teachers putting these on my tests if I did well. I like using them on cards and gifts.

No. 8924

Dennison

15¢

ST. PATRICK'S DAY SEALS

36 SEALS-6 DIFFERENT DESIGNS

FOR GIFTS, FAVORS, PLACE CARDS, & SCHOOL USE.

MADE IN U.S.A.

Antique shamrock lapel pins I found at an antiques show have tiny pipes, top hats, and even skeletons attached to them.

Central to my St. Patrick's Day decor, this vintage Hallmark honeycomb display is so joyful.

These vintage ceramic pixies are present in lots of my holiday displays. I especially like using them to decorate for St. Patrick's Day.

My partner's grandmother beaded this little pixie and attached him to a vase. It's now a sentimental addition to our St. Patrick's Day decor.

Easter

aster is a joyful holiday and a time to celebrate rebirth. For Christians, it's the time to celebrate the resurrection of Jesus Christ. Like most holidays, it's also very anchored in the season in which it resides, so of course it is also the celebration of spring coming after a long winter.

Just as the first crocuses, forsythia, and hyacinth begin to bloom, it's time for the Easter Bunny to come to town. Why do we have an Easter Bunny? Well, rabbits are known for their reproductive qualities, so they are a metaphor for life anew, which is at the heart of the season. This symbolism has roots in paganism, but like many other holidays, everything eventually got rolled under one umbrella with the heading of Easter. And certainly, the comparison could be drawn to the resurrection of Christ, so it all works.

In preparation for Easter, we dye eggs (my family does a special homemade dye from onion skins as well as the colorful versions), have Easter egg hunts, and don our best new pastels. For many years, it was also a time when women wore their new hats to church and to the Easter parade in just about every major city across the country.

As a kid, every Easter morning I'd wake to find all the eggs I'd dyed hidden all over the first floor of our house. I used to love scrambling (pun intended) to find them all. Mom got very creative in her hiding places, like inside a light fixture or behind a cushion. In fact, she was so creative that I'd invariably not find at least one, which we'd discover months later. I've compared notes with others who did this as a kid, and they had similar experiences. Holidays connect us!

In addition to finding the eggs, I'd also find a few Easter baskets made up for me with all kinds of treats and plastic eggs with coins or toys inside. One year my basket was a cowboy hat. I could take out all the goodies and wear it on Easter Day. How cool is that?

All this excitement happened before we even went to church services, which were always so very joyful. I loved seeing the sea of lilies (also a symbol of rebirth) and singing all the songs. Our pastor always had a special children's sermon, so we kids got to come down front and gather for a quick chat with him before the big sermon for the adults.

After church we'd head home, where Mom would start preparing a feast for us, including ham, pineapple filling, spinach pie, German potato salad, and much, much more. Considering she'd been up late filling Easter baskets and hiding those eggs, I now wonder how she did it all? I suppose love is like adrenaline—and Mom was definitely the Energizer Bunny on Easter.

For her efforts, we'd always give her potted tulips or hyacinths, which would wind up being planted in the yard. It's fun to see them come up every spring and know that each one was from an Easter of years past. In my home now, many pop up at this time of the year, and I smile to think of the past Easters so many celebrated here before me.

SIX WAYS I CELEBRATE A VERY VINTAGE EASTER

1. Carry on a tradition and/or start a new one.

Dying eggs was such a memorable and joyful part of my childhood, so of course I still do it as an adult. Depending on how many other things I have going on, at bare minimum I use those tablets and cups and dye the eggs vibrant solid colors. On years when I have more time, I do more-intricate painting. No matter how I do it, the idea is to have fun and enjoy those childhood memories involving yet another mindful vintage activity.

2. Use family decorations (or ones like them).

Mom had lots of ceramic Easter eggs and bunnies and several of those fun cardboard cutouts. I've found ones like them at flea markets that I now use and enjoy. Those chicks and bunnies connect me to my childhood and make my heart happy.

3. Make, bake, or mail something.

I've already talked about dying the eggs, so the other fun thing I like to create is Easter baskets for everyone. I like to use vintage baskets and that vintage grass, which I reuse every year. Inside I add all the goodies that Mom used to put in mine, like peanut butter eggs, foil-wrapped candy, and jelly beans. I also try to include little gifts that speak to each person's individual tastes.

© Getty Images/E+/GMVozd

4. Give your time and be present.

As I mentioned, when I was a kid, I loved church on Easter morning, and I still do. It is a wonderful way to honor my family's faith and connect to my childhood. While I hold the hymnal to sing the songs, I realize I don't really need it because I know them all by heart. There's something very comforting about that.

5. Share a meal.

Easter dinner is still a very big deal in my family, and Mom and Sis cook just like they did all those years ago. I love the savory ham with the sweet pineapple filling. Such a wonderful combo. On the table are pastel linens and my grandmother's Desert Rose china. Using her china is a way of still having her there with us. and it so very meaningful.

6. Do something interactive.

After a big meal, my family likes to take a walk together and then come back and play a game and watch a movie. For Easter we often play either *Pictionary* or *Taboo*, both of which have us laughing and enjoying the moment.

After dessert and coffee, we always watch *Easter Parade*. Judy Garland and Fred Astaire are a magical combination, and the musical numbers are still stunning to watch, even after a hundred viewings together as a family. I'm always amazed at Fred's energy and agility!

One year, to add to the celebration, we all wore funny vintage Easter bonnets I found at a vintage store. That made for lots of laughs and some great photos.

A VERY VINTAGE EASTER DECORATING

I love using vintage outdoor decorations inside, and I especially love when those items are handmade. This year I found a pair of giant hand-painted plywood rabbits that were originally created to be lawn decorations. When I found them at the flea market, I knew they would be the stars of my Easter display. I put them on either side of the tree in the kitchen, which is a bright green cellophane-feather tree given to me by my friend Bea.

I decorated the tree with vintage Italian lights that my friend Renee found for me. They were made for Christmas but are pastel and egg-shaped, so they are perfect for Easter. I then added some of my favorite mica-encrusted 1950s pastel Christmas ornaments, which, again, feel more like Easter than Christmas.

Around the tree I have an ever-growing collection of plastic and ceramic bunnies and chicks from all eras. I think they look like an ensemble cast of a musical. I also have cut flowers in vintage vases to add to the celebratory look. In front, I put people's baskets and a server with more wonderful dyed eggs.

Easter is a joyful holiday, and I want to make sure that comes across. In other rooms I also add branch and feather trees with hand-painted vintage wooden eggs. I put each in vintage flowerpots and jardinieres to add the look of spring.

Finally, I always have potted Easter plants like I give Mom every year. And just like the ones I give her, I plant mine in the yard after the holiday so they can come back for next Easter. It nicely underscores that message of rebirth!

Mom had this ceramic bunny basket on our dining room buffet every Easter. Now it's bringing joy to my home.

•❖•--------------------------------•❖•

Candy is key at Easter. I love these foil-covered dark chocolate eggs.

Easter baskets come in all sizes. I still make them for my loved ones, and this one features a foil-covered chocolate bunny and an antique cardboard egg filled with candy.

These small feather trees are perfect
for Easter with their pastel colors.
I love decorating them with vintage
hand-painted wooden eggs made
in Germany. I also display them in
vintage pottery flower pots and on
vintage display stands.

This little plastic Easter toy was
probably meant for a baby, as it has
seeds inside that rattle.

I added these lovely gold-leafed eggs to a midcentury egg tray for a pretty display.

These plastic bunnies are very cute and fit right in with my kitchen Easter display.

A handmade wooden Easter pull toy. I added some vintage grass and dyed eggs for a charming display.

This vintage papier-mâché container has one request: "Fill me with candy!"

I added a paper egg decoration to this happy rooster's wheelbarrow.

The color combinations on these kooky honeycomb decorations are decidedly late 1960s.

Wind-up vintage toys were made for most holidays. I love this one when it's in action. The umbrella twirls while it rolls along.

This cute Easter mailbox decoration features a very tiny chick.

Just like the toy above, this one spins and moves along joyfully.

I found this tiny bunny vase at an estate sale and added a fresh sprig of azalea from my backyard.

◦•◦ - ◦•◦

These three sassy plastic chicks were originally meant to hold lollipops.

This suite of antique German papier-mâché figures has tons of personality.

A chocolate bunny is always welcome at my house. This one's ceramic, painted to look like the real thing.

This tiny vintage tin toy is truly a thing of joy.

Before the egg hunt, this vintage ceramic bowl holds plastic eggs with toys, money, and candy inside.

I always gift plants at Easter, and when I do, I give them in vintage pots.

When my lilacs are in bloom at Easter, I cut some for display and for gifts (paired with a vintage vase).

Vintage candy boxes now make great display pieces, and I use them to store smaller decorations off-season.

This child's *Easter Parade* record is one I play every year, and I also love displaying the cover.

Mom had this cutout chick on our kitchen wall every year. Inexpensive decorations like these are commonly found at flea markets today.

A vintage battery-operated bunny lantern makes a great Easter night-light.

These German papier-mâché candy containers are so cute. The white one has springs attaching his ears, so they bounce when you open it.

Remember making things like this in art class for every holiday? I sure do.

Mom also had this cardboard bunny couple on our kitchen wall at Easter time. It's a favorite of mine.

This 1960s knee-hugger bunny boy is kooky and cute.

I love adding vintage seals like these to Easter cards.

Every year, without fail, I watch *Easter Parade*. Judy and Fred still light up the screen.

•▸------------------------------◂•

This bunny once held bubble bath. Now he's just cute on his own.

•▸------------------------------◂•

These Easter Egg trees decorated with hand-painted eggs look great in vintage pots.

Birthdays

MOTHER'S DAY / FATHER'S DAY

Birthdays are something just about everyone celebrates (whether they want to or not!), and I have many happy memories of birthday parties, both from my childhood and from my adulthood.

When I was a kid, Mom always made a special cake (typically her chocolate fudge triple-layer cake with chocolate frosting). It was the birthday cake my family loved, and Mom still makes it to this day. As I got older, she started asking me if I wanted to pick another cake for her to bake, and after much deliberation, I always went back to the chocolate one—and I typically still do. That said, my sister made me an orange cake recently that rocked my world, so I am now alternating from year to year!

My childhood also included many birthday parties with family and friends. Since I am a July baby, it was usually a picnic, and my cake was topped with sparklers. While I have vivid memories of the parties and the cakes and even some of the gifts, my favorite memories are when my brother came home from New York and join in the celebration. He always made me feel seen and celebrated—and that's the greatest gift of all for a kid (adults too!).

As an adult, I typically celebrate in smaller ways with a quiet dinner among family and friends. Like most holidays, for me it's really about celebrating with loved ones. In adulthood, I have also discovered the virtues of having more than one celebration. I think of my birthday as a time period . . . not just a day.

My dear friend Sharon and I have birthdays not too far apart, so we always get together and have a joint celebration and catch-up with just the two of us. With busy lives and overbooked schedules, it's so nice to make this a priority. With over three decades of friendship under our belts, we've celebrated a lot of birthdays, and these are moments I cherish.

When it comes to celebrating the birthdays of others, I have started using Mom's recipes and baking cakes. I also give primarily vintage gifts that I believe the recipients will appreciate for a variety of reasons. Vintage gifts are often very personal, even one-of-a-kind. Because of this, I shop for them all year long and buy them when I see them. If you're going to do this, take my advice and designate a spot where you put them all so you don't have to play that not fun game, "Where did I put that gift?" when a birthday rolls around.

SIX WAYS I CELEBRATE A VERY VINTAGE BIRTHDAY

1. Carry on a tradition and/or start a new one.

Whether it's my birthday or the birthday of a loved one, some traditional things always take place. First, there's always a cake (or two or three, depending on how many celebrations we're having). At least one of them is homemade. Then, of course, there are candles, singing "Happy Birthday," and wish-making. I can't think of a birthday when I've not had these things—without them, it just wouldn't feel like a birthday at all. Funny how these rituals and traditions have become so much a part of how we celebrate!

2. Use family decorations (or ones like them).

As a kid, I always had balloons on my birthday; I still do. I like giving them to people because they really tap into our childhood memories. I personally prefer the good old latex balloons blown up with helium and tied with color-coordinated curly ribbon.

Another vintage decorative item that's also functional is the plastic birthday candleholders everyone used to have. I love them, and they instantly ignite happy childhood memories. I have found them at flea markets and keep them washed and ready to use in a little bag with my stash of birthday candles. Every time I use them, I have visions of Mom's chocolate cake with them on top.

The truth is, we've become a bit lazy, and now people just put the candles directly in the cake. I, for one, really appreciate doing it the vintage way, and so do my loved ones. Plus, it's practical—you don't have to fish a burned-down candle out of the cake! *Note:* Today's candles might be a tad smaller than the ones made years ago, so you may need some of that sticky wax on the bottom of each holder to keep them in place.

3. Make, bake, or mail something.

Every year I am lucky enough to get at least two homemade cakes (one from my mom and sister and another from my partner). I have started baking them as well (thanks, Mom, for passing along your recipes!), and the tradition is really fun and satisfying. I love the idea of creating something from scratch, and since cooking and baking are acts of love, I am passing along the sentiment right along with the sweet.

Of course, cards are key for birthdays, and like all holidays, I often send vintage versions I find at flea markets. I still have many of mine from childhood, and it's fun to see the designs (and see who sent them). In fact, I often use them as part of my decorating so that these wonderful, tangible memories are part of my present day.

My friend Sharon makes cards and pieces of fine art, so I am always the lucky beneficiary of one of her latest designs. Each one is so beautiful, I pack it with my decor like the ones from my childhood so her creations can be ready to dazzle every year.

4. Give your time and be present.

Carving out time to really celebrate with loved ones is what a birthday celebration is all about. I like to highlight my gratitude for the fact that this person was born in this world at this time, as we are all better for it. It really is a celebration of someone's life—and their journey through the calendar for yet another year.

5. Share a meal.

Many people go out to a restaurant to celebrate their birthdays, and I certainly have been one of them. That said, the older I get, the more I appreciate being at home enjoying a home-cooked meal. Just like when I was a kid, many have been picnics, where I get to enjoy nature and the simple pleasures of flowers and woodland animals in my backyard.

6. Do something interactive.

Some of the favorite birthday gifts I've given and received have been those that are experiences. Whether it's a trip to a botanical garden, a museum, a theater, or a movie, I think it's fun to do something to commemorate the day. My favorite interactive thing of all to do? Go to a flea market or other vintage venue of course!

A VERY VINTAGE BIRTHDAY DECORATING

This year I decorated the kitchen for my joint birthday celebration with Sharon. I took my inspiration from children's parties from the 1940s and 1950s. I used colors like yellow, green, pink, and blue. I pulled them mostly from another set of wonderful kitchen curtains my sister Robin made for me from vintage material I found.

Since our joint celebration takes place in the summertime, I wanted it to feel like a picnic. I used a green artificial tree with vintage yellow lights and decorated it entirely with vintage plastic ornaments in the same colorway. Many of them are farm animals, which also adds to the summertime vibe. I put the whole thing in a vintage cooler I found at my local flea market (a nod to the picnic feel). Since the tree's in the kitchen, I decided to use a vintage potholder as a tree topper. Underneath, front and center, I added an advertising piece for Robin Hood shoes that is a lot of fun.

On either side, I used pottery, flowers, and a few cute decorations, like a blow-mold pig that was

likely a store advertising display, a ceramic pixie, and a felt doll to add a sense of playfulness. On the wall behind the tree, I used giant vintage nylon butterflies I got for fifty cents each at a thrift store.

Above it all is a sensational "Happy Birthday" sign my friend Chanelle found for me. I have seen signs like this (a faux bois font) saying "Merry Christmas," "Happy New Year," and even "Season's Greetings," but never "Happy Birthday," so I was excited to add it to my collection.

Of course our wrapped gifts are there waiting to be opened. I found the paper on a giant roll from a long-ago department store wrapping counter and have been using it for more than twenty years! And what birthday celebration would be complete without a cake and balloons?!

Both the cake and the balloons are in those same four colors, so while there is a lot going on in this display, it works because color harmonizes all of it—crazy as it may be! I couldn't wait to sit down, pour some coffee in the vintage cups and saucers, sing "Happy Birthday" to each other, and dig into that cake! Like so many of the things I aim to do, I feel like this display is an invitation to have fun, disconnect from the business of the outside world, and connect with each other. And what a gift that is!

Mother's Day and Father's Day

Mother's Day is one of the top holidays for greeting cards and flowers. When it was started in 1908 to honor mothers, retailers had a field day. A few years later, fathers got their day (unofficially)— Father's Day didn't become a national holiday until almost seventy years later. Better late than never, dads!

Breakfast in bed, dining out, and other fun activities honoring our parents are ripe with opportunities to share stories and photos and make memories.

While I don't decorate for these holidays, I do like to honor them with cards, gifts, and phone calls. I am grateful I get to do this with my mom and other women in my family.

While my dad was alive, I did this for him, but now that he's passed, I do these things for a gentleman who is like a father to me.

Although new cards are wonderful, I like to find great vintage cards for Mother's Day and Father's Day. There are many out there, and they are definitely smile-inducing!

As we grow older, I find parents just really want us to spend time with them, so many of the gifts I give are the ones that involve time and interaction (a meal, a road trip, a movie). Since those gifts can be challenging to wrap, I often give a vintage token to symbolize the gift. An hourglass, for example, symbolizes time (an afternoon together watching movies or playing games). A road map signifies a trip, so I like to give a vintage map or some sort of ephemera to emphasize that element.

Cut flowers are gifts I regularly give, and when I do, I always put them in vintage vases—the vase actually becomes part of the gift. It's also nice because the recipient doesn't have to do anything (like run and put the flowers in water); it's all done. Of course, flowers and vintage gifts are great for birthdays as well. Thoughtful, nostalgic gifts are always appreciated.

Vintage booklets like these are fun ways to both get ideas and spot now vintage ephemera to add to your collections.

Once upon a time everyone had birthday candleholders like these. I still use them.

Most people always had a box or two of birthday candles in a kitchen drawer. I love the look of these.

1950s cowgirl birthday candles in their original box are definitely too cute to burn and have great decorative value.

These circus-themed candleholders are on their original card with great graphics.

Vintage Happy Birthday cake toppers add a nice vintage touch to any confection.

Porcelain figures like this were often given as gifts to mark a specific birthday.

A fancy three-layer coconut cake is ideal for a birthday party. Vintage calendars and leaflets like these have wonderful old recipes and party ideas.

A vintage seal on a new birthday card or envelope adds a special touch. I buy these whenever I see them and use them to add a nostalgic element.

What mom wouldn't love a handmade card? This one has a little mirror inside.

•◦>------------------------------<◦•

Vintage Mother's Day and Father's Day cards are frame-worthy and make great gifts.

•◦>------------------------------<◦•

A vintage store sign I framed that nods to Father's Day.

CHAPTER

8

Independence Day

With summer in full swing, Independence Day is often celebrated with picnics and fireworks. Since the day commemorates the signing of the Declaration of Independence and, subsequently, the formation of the United States of America, it is a pretty big deal. It's the day we show our patriotism, fly our flag, and decorate with red, white, and blue.

As a kid, I was always out with my family in lawn chairs, watching the light display (while our poor pets hid under the bed and waited for it all to be over). Like many holidays, this activity had a way of helping us feel connected with everyone else who was doing the exact same thing.

We had sparklers at home, and I greatly enjoyed the excitement they brought into kiddom. I have a July birthday, so sparklers were always on my cake. (Try blowing *them* out!)

In addition to the display of the American flag, decorating also typically includes images of Uncle Sam. Uncle Sam, by the way, is generally regarded as the United States personified. He even has the same initials, and his ensemble pulls from all parts of the American flag.

Many, many decorative items were made to commemorate the US Bicentennial in 1976. I remember all these decorative objects from their first go-round; now they are vintage.

I decorate with these patriotic pieces, as well as just generally color-blocking with red, white, and blue objects. I have multiple patriotic trees with World War II–era plastic Christmas ornaments and other red, white, and blue ephemera.

With Easter far behind, I often decorate for Independence Day early and leave the decorations up for most of the summer.

SIX WAYS I CELEBRATE A VERY VINTAGE INDEPENDENCE DAY

1. Carry on a tradition and/or start a new one.

Most traditions I continue to keep alive were ones I knew from childhood, like picnics and fireworks, so both are always in order. If I'm traveling, I still uphold the tradition, just modify it a bit. This past year we were in Vermont, so we packed a picnic dinner, got to see and hear the Vermont Symphony Orchestra in an outdoor amphitheater, and enjoyed fireworks afterward.

2. Use family decorations (or ones like them).

Since I was a kid during the Bicentennial, decorating for the Fourth of July was commonplace. American flags; red, white, and blue colors; and Uncle Sam ephemera were in my childhood home and are now in my adult home. Because I decorate trees for this holiday, I often use vintage patriotic Christmas ornaments as well.

3. Make, bake, or mail something.

With berries in season, I like to go to a local farm and take advantage of their bumper crop. I use them to make blueberry muffins according to Mom's recipe. They are easy to serve and eat at a picnic, and a bite of one takes me back to happy childhood memories. They also freeze beautifully, so I make extra and keep them handy to take in the car for breakfast-on-the-go when I'm out early and off to summertime yard sales!

4. Give your time and be present.

Since I'm a pretty patriotic guy, and since this holiday is about celebrating the birth of our nation, I like to take friends and family to places like Philadelphia, Gettysburg, or Washington's Crossing (all in Pennsylvania close to my home) for some history and a bit more understanding of how exactly our country became the land of the free and home of the brave.

5. Share a meal.

Picnics are where it's at, and foods include all the general summertime salads, savory grilled meats, sun tea, and lemonade. It's fun to dine outside in a casual way, and I love using my vintage dishes, glassware, and linens—in a patriotic colorway, of course!

6. Do something interactive.

One game we always played on July 4 when I was a kid was beanbag (known to some as corn hole). Like many people, we had a homemade set of boards (made by my dad in his workshop) and beanbags in fun colors (made by my mom at our family business). Since I don't have those items any longer, I was delighted to find a patriotic hand-painted set at a flea market. Usually, we start playing on July 4 and keep it up all summer long.

Another fun thing to do on Independence Day is to watch *Yankee Doodle Dandy*, the story of George M. Cohan. James Cagney is great, and it always turns into a sing-along when that famous, catchy song comes on.

A VERY VINTAGE INDEPENDENCE DAY DECORATING

This is my first decorated holiday in a few months, so I usually decorate at least two trees—one in the kitchen and one in the bathroom. And since there's no more holiday decorating going on until Halloween, I leave the trees up most of the summer—one of them even longer.

For the kitchen I used a vintage silver tree, to which I added new small white lights. For a fun touch, I put the tree in a bicentennial potato chip can I found at a local antiques store. On the tree I added 1940s plastic ornaments in red and blue. Of course I used a vintage star for the topper. Draped around the tree is a vintage crepe paper streamer with little flags.

On either side of the tree, I displayed Uncle Sam figures and color-blocked red, white, and blue kitchen items. As a finishing touch, I added a couple of those cardboard cutout flags that used to be on the walls and windows of my classroom in grade school.

My bathroom is always decorated with a patriotic theme—primarily 1940s WWII-era vintage ephemera and decorative items. So all the items on the table were already in place. I just added a new red, white, and blue feather tree to the mix. I really wanted it to have a 1940s patriotic feel, so I used red and blue vintage lights with silver reflectors that have such a great look to them. I strung silver tinsel garland and added tiny American flags and stars that were meant for hors d'oeuvres. On top I used a handmade silver star. For the base I used a vintage patriotic toy drum my partner found for me at an antiques shop.

During the war years, patriotic Christmas decorations were very popular, and I collect them when I can find them. Since I typically decorate a couple patriotic trees every Christmas, I just leave this one up through year's end.

This chalkware trio is in my WWII-themed bathroom all year long. They were likely carnival prizes during the WWII years.

I love attaching these vintage seals to cards and packages.

No. 8918 · **Dennison** · 15¢

PATRIOTIC SEALS

36 SEALS-6 DIFFERENT DESIGNS

FOR GIFTS, FAVORS, PLACE CARDS, & SCHOOL USE.

MADE IN U. S. A.

A little vintage patriotic bling goes a long way. This pin is a favorite of mine.

What's a July 4th celebration without party hats? This one with stars, stripes, and raffia is a lot of fun.

• ❖ ┄┄┄┄┄┄┄┄┄┄┄┄┄┄┄┄┄┄┄┄┄┄ ❖ •

This vintage cardboard Liberty Bell wall decoration was in my classrooms every year when I was a kid. When I found it at a flea market, it brought back lots of memories.

An American flag on Independence Day really makes the point. Mine is vintage, and I found it in its original box.

This tall, slender Uncle Sam blow mold decoration holds a small American flag.

Typical of the merchandise made to commemorate America's Bicentennial, this Uncle Sam figure and plastic bank are a lot of fun.

200 YEARS

Cardboard flag decorations like this were typically used to decorate classrooms all over the country.

Like all holidays, Independence Day has a soundtrack. These vintage records are always playing on my stereo every year.

This vintage giveaway booklet was a gift from my friend Matthew. It has great graphics and interesting historical information.

A trio of vintage plastic stars, these WWII-era ornaments are perfect for my patriotic trees.

This antique postcard underscores the celebratory nature of Independence Day.

A kitschy handmade Betsy Ross doll, this was likely created around America's Bicentennial.

•❖•--------------------------------------•❖•

Giving a gift on July 4th? Why not wrap it in vintage paper?!

•❖•--------------------------------------•❖•

These antique patriotic Christmas ornaments look great on my patriotic trees.

Since my birthday is close to Independence Day, Mom always put sparklers on my cake. I use these vintage boxes as part of my decorating now, as they bring back lots of good memories.

Another cute patriotic piece made around the Bicentennial, this Liberty Belle was a fun flea market find.

The graphics on this WWII-era toy drum are wonderful.

My friend Chanelle gave me this great box of unused WWII-era patriotic cards. They are a now a treasured part of my collection.

Halloween

Halloween is another holiday awaited with great anticipation—magical and fun for kids of all ages. Just like Christmas, it's a time when our inner child can come out and play. As long as I can remember, it was a big deal to plan my costume—it still is! I had some memorable costumes, some homemade and some store bought. Wearing them to school and taking part in a parade were always highlights.

Like so many of our holidays, Halloween has its roots in Celtic celebrations; trick-or-treating and carving pumpkins are a couple of the things that can be traced back to them. The name Halloween (sometimes spelled "Hallowe'en,") is taken from All Hallows' Eve, the night before All Hallows' Day (or All Saints' Day), a Catholic holiday that honors all saints and falls on November 1.

Trick-or-treating as we know it today began in an organized fashion in the 1930s to keep kids out of mischief on Halloween night. The idea was to give them treats so they didn't play tricks (or pranks). In my kid world, trick-or-treating was an annual highlight, and for me the best part was my big brother taking me out. One year my homemade costume (an upside-down man creatively fashioned by my mom) fell apart after school. My brother, Johnny, stepped in at the last minute and used his own hat and clothing to make me a woodsman. He rouged my cheeks and grabbed an old ax from the basement as finishing touches. Funnily enough, sans the rouge and the ax, I still kind of dress like a woodsman to this very day. When you shine light upon a child, it can have powerful and lasting results.

TV screen image © Getty Images/Moment/Marianna Armata

Just like the special Christmas tree Johnny decorated for me in my room, making me a costume and taking me trick-or-treating were gifts of his creativity and time. For me, they are gifts that keep on giving. I still have the card he sent me from college in New York, letting me know he was coming home to spend Halloween with me. A Hallmark *Peanuts* card, I keep it tucked in my china cabinet all year long—any time I want to see his writing or be reminded of that powerfully happy memory, I can just take it out for a quick look.

So, yes, like all holidays, even Halloween has a sentimental vibe for me. The same goes for how I decorate. My Halloween decor is all about being cute rather than scary. Life can be scary enough. I have an enormous amount of happy blow-mold jack-o'-lanterns, die-cut wall decorations, and more—all of which remind me of things my mom had or were used to decorate our classroom in school.

Carving the jack-o'-lanterns is an annual event. It's another one of those mindful vintage activities.

Did you know that the origin of carving jack-o'-lanterns was reportedly to ward off evil spirits? For those who believe in the mysticism of Halloween, it is said that the veil between the spirit world and ours is very thin on October 31, so that jack-o'-lantern can be used to ward off any unwanted spirits in your home. While you're at it, you can also light a white candle (or turn on a white LED tea candle) and welcome in the friendly spirits—like Casper!

SIX WAYS I CELEBRATE A VERY VINTAGE HALLOWEEN

1. Carry on a tradition and/or start a new one.

I live in a town where we take trick-or-treating very seriously. Thousands of kids come to show off their costumes and fill up on candy. As far as I can recall, Halloween is the only holiday where we open our doors to strangers (other than Christmas carolers). As a kid, I was the one with the bag going door to door. Now I'm at the door handing out candy—and, I have to say, I think it's even more fun!

It is, indeed, more blessed to give than to receive, and that doesn't just go for Christmas. While I know the kids come for the candy, I know it means something to them and to their parents to have their costume praised. Spending a night doing this for literally thousands of kids is a grand tradition I have grown to love.

TRICK-OR-TREAT!

I don't just hand out candy and praise costumes. I also decorate my porch and plan a special costume for each year. Since my best friend, Sharon, is a very talented visual and makeup artist, I get the royal treatment when it comes to costumes.

Just like my brother, Johnny, and Mom did for me when I was a kid, Sharon creates costumes for me as an adult. Each year I get theatrical makeup and a special ensemble. It puts a spring in my step and definitely puts me in the Halloween mood!

2. Use family decorations (or ones like them).

I mentioned those ceramic jack-o'-lanterns earlier. Even though Mom's broke and was tossed years ago, I enjoy displaying the ones I've found at flea markets. They bring back happy memories of that one I loved as a kid. The same goes for my many vintage blow-mold decorations and cardboard cutouts. None of them actually belonged to my mom, but all remind me of the one that did. Comfort, connection, and continuity!

3. Make, bake, or mail something.

Carving pumpkins is something my partner and I do together every year. Again, it's mindful, and we each get to express our creativity and have some fun and laughter along the way. We even scoop out the seeds, rinse them off, and roast them with some cinnamon and sugar in the oven. It makes the house feel cozy and warm, and they taste great!

Bob's Halloween Movie Picks

THE BRIDE OF FRANKENSTEIN

This classic film introduces a pop-culture icon, fantastically portrayed by Elsa Lanchester. She was the first female monster, and instead of being hideous, she's actually beautiful, which was very much intentional! While I also love *Frankenstein*, I like this one even better. Like *Frankenstein*, it's a social commentary and includes fine performances, revolutionary makeup artistry, and much, much more.

I MARRIED A WITCH

Long before *Bewitched* came to TV, this movie showed audiences that a witch could be beautiful and not at all scary. Starring Veronica Lake, this comedy is also a social commentary and a wildly enjoyable farce. It weaves in a bit of history, a bit of magic, and a lot of laughs.

ARSENIC AND OLD LACE

Directed by Frank Capra of *It's a Wonderful Life* fame, this movie is a real gem. It's based on a hit play and is a great mix of screwball comedy and dark humor. Cary Grant is hilarious, and the supporting cast are all superb. Like *It's a Wonderful Life*, it also has heart (which is why I love it, of course). The opening credits have fun vintage Halloween graphics that are a treat to see.

Like I do for all major holidays, I send cards to loved ones. Often I send vintage ones I've found at flea markets.

4. Give your time and be present.

Back to trick-or-treating. Doling out candy to thousands of kids is an activity that keeps me very much in the moment. My partner and friends like Sharon help with candy and crowd control. It is very much a team effort—and the stuff great Halloween memories are made of!

5. Share a meal.

Each year after trick-or-treating ends, my neighbor hosts a big potluck party where we all share stories of the night and admire one another's costumes. Everybody brings something yummy; it's a great time to try new things, exchange recipes, and celebrate Halloween in a connected way.

6. Do something interactive.

It doesn't get more interactive than the trick-or-treating night I described, but I do like to make popcorn and other snacks and watch a good Halloween movie with loved ones. While there are so many super-scary, gory movies with Freddie and Jason and Michael terrorizing people, I prefer the classic horror films of the 1930s like *Frankenstein*, *The Bride of Frankenstein*, etc. Since I have a cool 1949 TV that's been refurbished by my friends at a wonderful store called Vintage Vibe, the movies feel even more authentic.

TV screen image © Getty Images/Moment/Marianna Armata

Here are a few of my favorite Halloween costumes. I still get as excited about dressing up as I did when I was a kid. That's also me as Scooby Doo (opposite page).

A VERY VINTAGE HALLOWEEN DECORATING

As I mentioned in chapter 1, I used a lot of orange and black in my living room to give the Halloween feel. While many items are vintage Halloween decorations, I also assembled orange and black pottery and glass, candles, and more.

Since the living room is where we gather to watch Halloween movies, I like the whole space to feel warm and have continuity. Color does this, along with a steady mix of vintage pieces chosen from my collection.

My TV is from 1949, but not everything in the room hails from that period. I have furniture, home furnishings, and Halloween decorations from lots of eras, but because I arrange by color and shape, it all works.

I had a lot of fun adding a fabric hand to the TV, as well as a vintage ceramic store-display hand to an old box for a spooky but playful look. A vintage black telephone and a vintage orange one also came in from other rooms to add to the fun.

In addition, I used a vintage Halloween trick-or-treat bucket to hold a pepper plant and hung silk leaves around all the windows. They added that bit of nature I like to include and allowed me to use some old things in new ways.

In the dining room, I used vintage Christopher Radko ornaments on a pre-lit twig tree that makes an

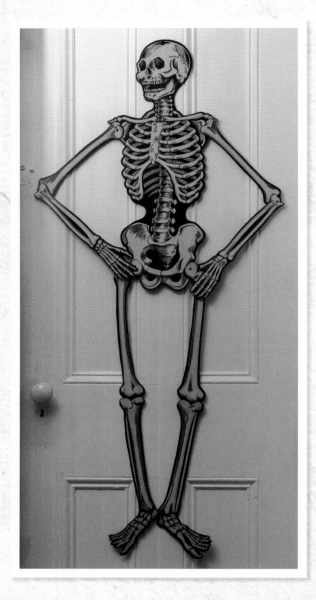

appearance there for most holidays. A huge vintage cardboard skeleton hangs on one door, while cardboard jack-o'-lanterns, owls, and more adorn other areas.

My vintage tablecloth has a wonderful warm orange glow, and it really comes to life when I add 1930s black porcelain candlesticks and a bowl of apples from a local farm. On the other sideboard, I have vintage ceramic ghosts that continue to multiply as I add more whenever I find them at flea markets and my local thrift store.

The kitchen is where I have fun with some of my favorite Halloween blow molds. Although typically associated with outdoor decor, I like using these decorations inside. When they are all lit, the kitchen takes on a warm, orange glow that makes me very happy—an unexpected side benefit of using these decorations inside.

Blow molds can be a challenge to arrange, since they are intended to sit on a flat surface. I created an asymmetrical display this year by hanging some on the wall, placing others atop canisters, and then putting the rest directly on the kitchen island. I love how they look together—a collage of sorts. The curtains my sister made from vintage 1930s floral fabric I found are the perfect backdrop.

All in all, like my decorating for all the bigger holidays, my Halloween decor evolves and changes from year to year (and sometimes day to day!). My touchstone is that I want it to feel fun and playful rather than creepy or scary.

This black cat in a jack-o-lantern is one of the largest blow molds in my collection.

Another favorite vintage blow mold, this owl loves to hang around my home at Halloween.

I call this my "million pumpkin wreath." I found it at a local shop and added a vintage paper cat wall decoration for a vintage touch.

Light-up jack-o-lanterns like this were frequently painted in ceramics classes in the 1970s. This fellow has crushed glass crystals that add a special touch.

Battery-operated lanterns like this could be used as decorations or to light the way for trick-or-treaters.

I love the simplicity of this vintage ceramic light jack-o-lantern. There are so many varieties out there.

A vintage Halloween paper plate I found in my travels. Ephemera like this is fun to collect and display.

I remember getting bags like these filled with candy from my trick-or-treating days.

This antique place card is actually hand-painted. It's a favorite piece in my collection.

These antique German die-cut decorations are some of the oldest Halloween pieces in my collection. They are thicker than other paper pieces out there, and many have stands on the back so they can be used on a tabletop as well as on the wall.

This antique German jack-o-lantern decoration is another favorite piece of mine.

This vintage acetate Halloween doily is frame-worthy.

When it comes to entertaining, I love using vintage pieces like these nut cups and witch candy container.

Candles that were just too cute to burn were made for just about every holiday by a company called Gurley. These two are favorites in my Halloween collection.

Vintage Halloween noisemakers are both fun and functional.

These vintage Halloween costumes are still in their original boxes.

These vintage light up jack-o-lantern blowmolds are very nostalgic. So many of us had them in our childhood homes. Now I find them at flea markets and enjoy displaying them together.

The blow mold treat pail has room for lots of goodies and looks great with a battery-operated LED tea light inside.

These happy vintage light-up
Halloween blow molds definitely fall
under the category of "cute" rather
than scary. I love arranging them
together and using them both inside
and outside.

An orange ghost candle, too cute to ever be burned, is a favorite object of mine.

A vintage Halloween candy container with the candy still inside.

This knee-hugger jack-o-lantern is a distant cousin of those Christmas elves we all know and love.

This bell noisemaker is rare and has great graphics.

This vintage Hallmark jack-o-lantern honeycomb lampshade cover has become a much-loved addition to my Halloween decor.

Vintage magazines and pamphlets I've found at flea markets have given me great inspiration for decorating and entertaining.

A vintage party plate with amazing graphics.

This battery-operated plastic jack-o-lantern has eyes that light up.

Little vintage toys like this make great decorative touches.

This tiny vintage makeup powder container is now a great piece of Halloween decor.

These old crepe paper Halloween
decorations have strings attached
for hanging and were likely used as
Halloween party decorations.

Antique Halloween party favors like
these are rare and wonderful. I love
the paper cutouts on them.

A wonderful antique Halloween
postcard from my dear friend Julia.

More vintage blow molds. The top two light up with a nightlight bulb. The bottom jack-o-lantern is a treat bucket. I put a battery-operated LED tea light inside to make it glow.

A fun plastic Halloween pull toy, this fellow is pure joy.

• ❯ - ❮ •

Pulp paper jack-o-lanterns like this were often used to light the way for trick-or-treaters. Now they are prized by collectors.

• ❯ - ❮ •

These little plastic Halloween toys squeak when you open them.

I love vintage black glass pieces like this bottle with silver stars. They make great vases for flowers at Halloween.

⬧- -⬧

This vintage plastic lollipop holder is another cute container for candy or flowers.

⬧- -⬧

I use this black glass flower frog to display my collection of vintage Halloween cupcake picks.

These two German Halloween candy containers are favorite pieces in my collection.

Here's a very nostalgic, fun Halloween record that many remember from childhood. I still play it at parties and when trick-or-treaters come.

This vintage piece of artwork probably had a place of honor on a proud mom's refrigerator many moons ago.

A handmade trick-or-treat bag has lots of charm and sentimental value.

My Aunt Viv used to make Halloween cookies in these shapes. I loved them, and I also love the box.

A vintage Halloween party napkin that's now frame-worthy.

• ❯ ------------------------------- ❮ •

This jack-o-lantern is actually a battery-operated lantern. I love his spring appendages.

• ❯ ------------------------------- ❮ •

Another vintage paper booklet with great ideas and inspiration.

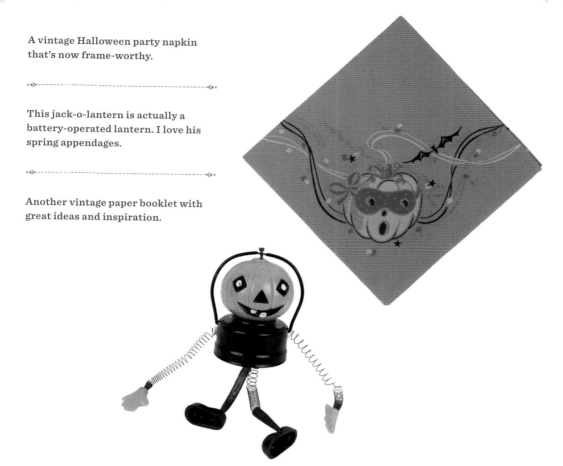

A sweet ceramic scarecrow is a welcome addition to my collection.

• ‹ ›————————————————————‹ ›•

I like to display this vintage blow mold witch noisemaker in a black glass vase.

• ‹ ›————————————————————‹ ›•

This little ceramic jack-o-lantern vase is super cute.

• ‹ ›————————————————————‹ ›•

The top comes off this large blow mold jack-o-lantern, so he can be used to store candy.

This trio of hand-painted jack-o-lantern businessmen makes me smile.

These large cardboard owl decorations from the 1950s can be found at flea markets and antiques venues. They make a big impact hung in my dining room.

I found this little 1960s witch at a local thrift store and she flew home with me.

CHAPTER 100

Thanksgiving

A whole holiday that is all about gratitude! How can that not be a great thing? When I was growing up, it was a greatly anticipated holiday because we always had special foods served in the same bowls and on the same trays. The smell of Mom's turkey and filling (some call it stuffing or dressing) wafted through the house, and it is a scent I strongly associate with home. Each year when I walk through the door and catch a whiff of it, I am instantly comforted and excited at the same time.

From soup (Mom always makes pumpkin) to nuts (mixed and served in a green Depression glass dish) and everything in between (like that big, juicy turkey), it is an annual feast I look forward to each year. In fact, according to my mom, I used to write home from college requesting all the items on the menu (like she wasn't going to make them anyway!).

Pumpkin pie is paramount. Mom's is more of a custard, and it's my favorite—an old recipe she got from my grandmother, who got it from a good friend. (See chapter 13 for the recipe.)

There are numerous conflicting stories about the first Thanksgiving, but what is common to all of them is that the meal itself celebrated the bounty of the harvest. With gratitude at the epicenter of this holiday, in addition to a prayer usually offered up by yours truly, my family goes around the table, with each member sharing something for which we are grateful that year. Often, it is just for being heathy and together—and of course there's always a thank-you for the food.

For some, the holiday has evolved into "Friendsgiving" and is a potluck meal for families we create. No matter how large or small the scale, there always seems to be great food and lots of it. Table settings, centerpieces, and good china are all part of the day; and for me, they are about having fun with vintage tableware I've found on my vintage shopping excursions.

As for other decor, of course there's a Thanksgiving tree filled with preserved leaves (described more in the next section), vintage wall decor, and even a blow-mold turkey.

SIX WAYS I CELEBRATE A VERY VINTAGE THANKSGIVING

1. Carry on a tradition and/or start a new one.

As a kid, I used to pick up beautiful autumn leaves and then come home and press them between the pages of a book to preserve them. And there they'd often stay. Then one day I learned how to preserve leaves with a warm iron, two pieces of waxed paper, and a tea towel. I'm sure Nana or Mom taught me, but I don't recall the first time I did it.

Years went by, and as I got older, I stopped preserving leaves. Well, now I've started again—and let me tell you, it is something I really love. It connects me to my childhood and adds that natural element to my decorating that I love. I typically do this in the weeks leading up to Thanksgiving and use the leaves as part of my displays.

2. Use family decorations (or ones like them).

My mom had a pair of ceramic pilgrims that were always on the sideboard in the dining room. She still uses them, so I found a similar set at a flea market. The same goes for those cardboard cutouts Mom had on the kitchen wall (cornucopias, leaves, etc.). I found their vintage counterparts and love using them to decorate. They are a nod to my childhood and bring back a lot of good memories.

ANN PAGE
Pure Ground
ALLSPICE

ANN PAGE
Pure Ground
GINGER

GLOVES

PUMPKIN PIE SPICE

THU   NOV

24

The greater
the trials, the
more glorious
the triumph.

LOUIS F. DOW CO.

3. Make, bake, or mail something.

My mom and sister are in charge of the food on Thanksgiving, and they have shared all the recipes with me. That said, I learn by doing, and this year Mom showed me how to make her gravy. There are so many nuances that are not in a recipe (oh, and she doesn't even have a recipe for gravy—it's just in her head), so having her show me this year was both fun and educational.

For my partner's family, we made his grandmother's matzo ball soup for everyone, and it was really fun to learn how to do this as well. As we made it, I heard stories and enjoyed learning to make something that brings him comfort, connection, and continuity.

4. Give your time and be present.

Old-fashioned visiting is something that's central to Thanksgiving. I look forward to putting down the cell phone and connecting in an authentic way. I find that it's a very joyous day, and when mouths aren't filled with food, it's a great time to both catch up and reminisce.

Donating time, food, or funds to one of many charitable organizations is another wonderful way to say an energetic "thank-you" for all the gifts we've been given. I find that any sort of volunteerism always seems to help me more than those I'm helping. It helps broaden my perspective and reminds me of how very blessed I am.

5. Share a meal.

Dining together is what Thanksgiving is all about. And since there's so much food, we have many subsequent meals after the main one. In fact, Thanksgiving leftovers top my list of favorite menu items. For years we'd have a second Thanksgiving at my house the day after Thanksgiving at my mom's house. Since there's so much food, why not spread it out over several days and celebrations?

6. Do something interactive.

I have my live Christmas trees delivered the Wednesday before Thanksgiving, so every Thanksgiving night after the big meal, I start lighting them. My partner helps me unravel lights while I climb the ladder and start weaving them in and out of the branches. While doing this, we always watch the original *Miracle on 34th Street* (1947). The movie opens with the Macy's Thanksgiving Day Parade, so it seems only fitting to watch it on Thanksgiving night. If you've not seen this classic, give it a watch. It's all in there. And Edmund Gwenn won an Academy award for his pitch-perfect portrayal of Kris Kringle.

A VERY VINTAGE THANKSGIVING DECORATING

On the heels of Halloween, and with Christmas right around the corner, Thanksgiving can get lost in the decorating shuffle.

I concentrate my Thanksgiving decor in the dining room and kitchen (the two rooms where we all spend the most time during this holiday season).

I often recycle some of my Halloween decorations like silk leaves, pre-lit twig trees, etc., and since there's a similar color palette, it works organically.

What I always add are copious amounts of pumpkins, gourds, and mums, which I find at my wonderful local farmers' market. Many times I go with an idea of how many and what colors I'd like, but often I let what I find guide me as well. This year I found that I liked the yellow pumpkins and a few orange, yellow, and green variegated ones, so they came home with me. Because I like a traditional pumpkin-colored pumpkin (or two or three), I bought several of them as well. And so yellow, green, and pumpkin became my colors in the dining room.

I decorated the tree on my large buffet with vintage orange Christmas balls and the leaves I'd pressed. On top, I added a vintage felt sprite I found at a flea market. On either side I have vintage turkey candy containers, candles, and pottery figures in graduated heights. On my smaller buffet,

I had fun with a vintage Italian art pottery corn topiary I found at another vintage venue. This is one holiday when I really like playing out the metaphor of celebrating the harvest, and I used a lot of those pumpkins and gourds to make the point.

To play out the point even further, I filled a vintage ceramic cornucopia with various fruits from the grocery store. I added a bit of bittersweet as well to give it a bit more panache. I was very happy with the result, and it became a centerpiece on my dining table for many weeks in November leading up to Thanksgiving.

Of course my dining table is set with vintage china. I have several collections, so I like to mix and match and alternate from year to year. This year I chose a vintage French set from the 1960s with a wide green stripe. I added some older pieces and silverware that came from my partner's grandmother. One of my favorite items to add was the 1930s water goblets that belonged to my nana. I love the way they feel in my hand, and I truly believe that the water just tastes better in them.

Lastly, on a side table, I have the hat my friend Sharon made for my "Gentleman of the Woods" Halloween costume. That ensemble felt very autumnal, and the hat itself is a work of art. Next to it is a drawing Sharon did for another version of the same character. This display feels celebratory and whimsical, and makes me smile every time I walk by it.

Flanking my kitchen island are a "new" set of curtains made by my sister, who cut down and altered a vintage set I found at the flea market. I pulled from the colors and added pumpkins, bittersweet, and several fun items, like a large 1950s plaid cooler, a 1970s light-up ceramic owl, and a fantastic blow-mold plastic turkey, front and center. The framed vintage still life hanging above the island is a favorite piece, and it seemed to fit the overall theme of abundance.

Like my dining room display, the kitchen is also a celebration of the harvest and a joyful nod to this beautiful time of the year. In many ways I think of it as an altar of gratitude for my many blessings.

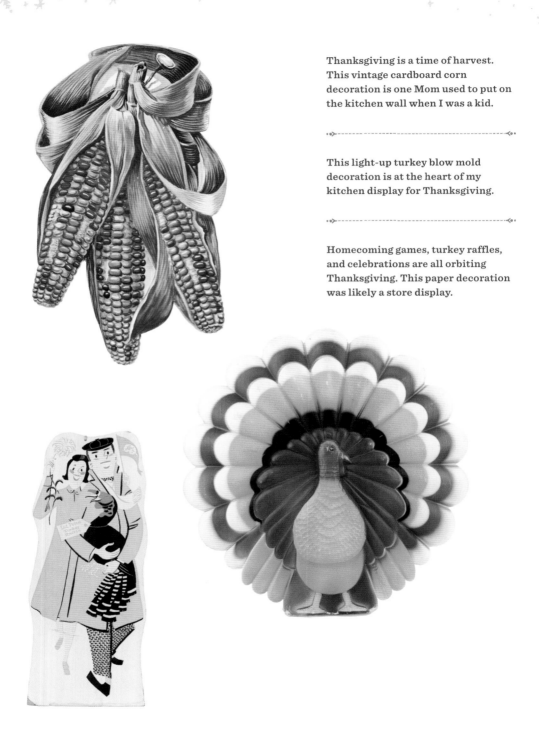

Thanksgiving is a time of harvest. This vintage cardboard corn decoration is one Mom used to put on the kitchen wall when I was a kid.

This light-up turkey blow mold decoration is at the heart of my kitchen display for Thanksgiving.

Homecoming games, turkey raffles, and celebrations are all orbiting Thanksgiving. This paper decoration was likely a store display.

More holiday candles that were just too cute to burn, this trio is familiar to many and easy to find at flea markets.

Handmade cards are the best and are typically saved by loving moms and family members.

This antique Thanksgiving postcard features some super cute anthropomorphic nuts.

This ceramic turkey cookie jar is always on display in my kitchen at Thanksgiving.

An antique Thanksgiving postcard featuring a patriotic theme.

This cardboard turkey cutout is typical of the ones I remember from my classrooms as a kid.

Nothing says kitschy like googly eyes!
I love this handmade wooden turkey
decoration.

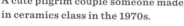

This German papier-mâché turkey
candy container has beautiful hand-
painted details.

A cute pilgrim couple someone made
in ceramics class in the 1970s.

This tiny ceramic open book is hand-painted and was likely a decoration for a place setting.

The autumnal colors of this vintage platter make it an easy addition to my Thanksgiving table.

The handle on this giant antique serving piece may have broken off a century ago, but someone mended it with wire and glue. I love displaying it with my Thanksgiving china.

Some of my decorations like this vintage ceramic scarecrow cross over from Halloween to Thanksgiving.

This flint corn candle and its vintage holder makes a fun table decoration.

A vintage toy wagon becomes a fun part of my Thanksgiving decor with a few pumpkins from the local farmers' market added.

This 1960s honeycomb Thanksgiving table decoration is a lot of fun.

The actual pumpkin in this vintage can is long gone, but the great label makes it a wonderful object to display.

Gifting mums is always nicer when you bring them in a vintage pot.

I found this old bottle with a Mayflower label and filled it with water and a few drops of orange food coloring. It makes a charming display piece.

•◦•------------------------------------◦•

Mom had both of these vintage cardboard Thanksgiving decorations on the kitchen wall when I was growing up. They have lots of emotional value for me.

Vintage pamphlets like this one are great resources for ideas on decorating the vintage way. Plus they just look great as part of holiday decor.

Once upon a time many people played bridge. These tallies were never used and have great graphics. I like to use them as place cards for my Thanksgiving table.

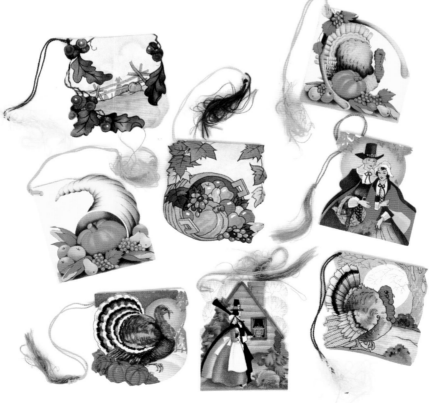

Mixing and matching china patterns is fun and easy, especially if you stick with one basic color. These three pieces of antique stoneware in shades of brown look great together.

This vintage cake stand is great for display and to serve any sweet treats.

Vintage spice tins like these have become very collectible. I love the colors and graphics.

DISCLAIMER: I believe in Santa Claus. As a child, when I left out milk and cookies for him and carrots for his reindeer, they were gone in the morning! My brother, Johnny, told me to do this, and it proved to me that Santa was real. That's all I needed. When I asked my sisters Robin and Jody if they'd ever seen Santa, they said they had not, but they did catch a glimpse of his reindeer once. Again, that was good enough for me. Now it's my job to keep the spirit of Santa Claus alive for future generations (and those of us who are eternal kids at heart).

Christmas / Hanukkah

I grew up going to church every Sunday. My favorite month was December, when we celebrated Advent, lighting a candle for each passing week that brought us closer to Christmas, which is all about celebrating the birth of Jesus Christ. Along with Easter (celebrating Christ's rebirth), Christmas is one of the most joyful times in the Christian faith in which I was raised. At home, Santa Claus was right there, front and center, in our celebrating as well, even though—just like the Easter Bunny and Easter—he really has nothing to do with the Christmas story I learned in church.

Santa does, however, have a connection to Christianity, as he evolved from Saint Nicholas, who was known for giving gifts to the poor. In fact, Saint Nicholas is even credited with inventing the Christmas stocking. As the story goes, he tossed gold into the window of a home where a poverty-stricken family lived, and some landed in the stockings that were hung up by the fire to dry. So Santa Claus is basically our Americanized version of Saint Nicholas—a physical representation of generosity and kindness of heart.

And, yes, I believe in the spirit of Santa Claus, and anyone who knows me knows that Christmas is my favorite holiday. I even wrote a whole book about it (*A Very Vintage Christmas*)! My childhood Christmases were filled with magic and wonder, and lots of amazing ornaments, lights, and decorations. They all had a powerful impact on me.

Some gifts I'll always cherish (both in memory and in tangible mementos) include a decorated tree from my brother, vintage ornaments from my dad, and learning from my mom and sister how to make my own ornaments. All these decorations just couldn't fit on one tree, so by the time I was about ten, we had at least three trees. And the number kept growing from there.

It was also about that time that my mom decided to let me do the decorating. I suppose she figured that if I wanted that many trees, then I should decorate them. I'm so grateful my mom saw my passion and let me express it. She never curbed my zeal but rather empowered me to run with it. What a great gift that was. It truly shaped who I grew up to become.

A Very Vintage Christmas taps into the childlike wonder and enthusiasm I have around the holidays, and it features my home and thousands of ornaments, lights, and decorations I display there.

Since I wrote that book, I'm now up to more than twenty trees each year—and counting. Just about every surface has some sort of holiday razzle-dazzle. Similarly, I've expanded my collection of decorations, so I've included many of my new favorites in this chapter.

My vintage trees include ones that are color-blocked and others that have themes (like WWII, American, homemade, and more). In this book, I'll zero in on favorite ornaments like the ones made during WWII, as well as homespun decor like popcorn and cranberries and paper chains. Again, doing these things connects us to the past and gives us a chance to slow down and be mindful.

I have my trees delivered the day before Thanksgiving so they have a chance to breathe and settle in. The scent is amazing and lets me know Christmas is coming. While many people are out shopping on Black Friday, I'm at home lighting my trees. Like all good things, it's a process that takes

time. I start on Thanksgiving night, and it usually goes on for several days. I use lots and lots of lights and weave them in and out of the branches to achieve a luminous, multidimensional look. Like so many of the things I do, I love the outcome more than the process, so I have found ways to make the process more enjoyable. In fact, I've found that there's something quite meditative about lighting a Christmas tree. I have done some great thinking while tree lighting and have grown to enjoy the time it takes.

Music plays a huge role in my Christmas celebrating. I always have Christmas records on while I'm decorating. I have so many Christmas albums. Remember those Firestone records? I have the ones that belonged to my family, and I still play them. Plus, I have amassed so many others that I really could have my own Christmas radio station (one idea that came to me while tree lighting!).

In chapter 1 I spoke about my great love for the album *John Denver and The Muppets: A Christmas Together*" and shared some favorite lyrics from the song "A Christmas Wish." There's another one called "Alfie The Christmas Tree/It's in Every One of Us" that always has me smiling and crying at the same time. In short, the song underscores the idea that **Christmas is love**. When we love more and judge less, we are embodying the spirit of Christmas. The same goes for giving versus receiving. Finding just the right gifts for everyone is something that brings me great joy.

Speaking of gifts, here's a great idea: Why not consider the gift of memories? Give some tangible objects that conjure up memories, like vintage ornaments or decorations that might have been on someone's grandmother's tree long ago. People absolutely love receiving them. Another idea is to gift activities that are reminiscent of a simpler time, like ice skating and hot chocolate, a historic house tour, or a Christmas concert. I love holiday activities, and I find there's never enough time to do all the ones I want to do. Some of the greatest gifts I've received are experiential, like these activities.

Decorating can also conjure up memories and make new ones. This year I brought back a favorite childhood activity: stringing popcorn and cranberries. It reminded me of so many Christmases doing the same thing with my mom. Now I do it in my home and make new memories while enjoying those old ones.

Speaking of my mom, one of her vintage activities I've kept alive is putting cloves in an orange and making pomanders to add a beautiful, fragrant touch to my holiday decor. Like most moms, mine was always going a mile a minute—cooking, baking, wrapping, decorating, shopping, etc. The last thing she'd do on Christmas Eve would be to sit at the dining room table and make a few orange-and-clove pomanders. Now I do the same thing. It's become a ritual that helps me slow down and honor that Christmas has arrived.

SIX WAYS I CELEBRATE A VERY VINTAGE CHRISTMAS

1. Carry on a tradition and/or start a new one.

While I carry on lots of Christmas traditions, one that means a great deal to me is attending church services on Christmas Eve. As a child it was so magical to dress up, sing all the songs, and be part of this joyful celebration. Back then, I was in the children's choir and played Joseph in the

annual pageant. These memories and many more come back to me each year when I'm in church celebrating the arrival of the Christ Child.

As an adult I attend Christmas Eve services; I still hold the hymnal, but I don't really need it. All those songs are already inside me. I especially love when we sing "Silent Night," each holding a candle in the darkened church. I always shed a few tears during that song. Knowing that millions of others around the world are having a similar experience makes me very happy. Just as that happiness crests, we blow out our candles as the lights come up, and we all sing "Joy to the World." By the end of the service, my heart is full.

When I get home, I usually still have some wrapping to do (typically the stocking stuffers), and I watch *It's a Wonderful Life*. While I love and watch many holiday movies every year, I always save this one for Christmas Eve, since that's when it takes place—and since I need to have my annual sob fest under the tree.

Last but not least, I put cloves in some oranges, just like Mom does. It is instant aromatherapy and lets all my senses know that Christmas has arrived.

On Christmas Day there are too many traditions to name here, but one I love is to add the Christ Child to the manger. Many churches do this. The entire manger scene is set up weeks before Christmas, except for the Babe, who is not born until Christmas Day. I like doing it as another little mindful activity.

After that, it's stockings and presents, a big breakfast, and an even bigger dinner. Oh, and lots of cookies in between!

Once I shared a Christmas dinner with a friend's family. After the meal, they all gathered around a large nativity figure of Jesus in the middle of the table and sang "Happy Birthday" to him. I thought that was such a fun thing. I love hearing about everyone's own special traditions. There are so many wonderful traditions; I often adopt some and add them to my ever-growing list of ways I celebrate.

2. Use family decorations (or ones like them).

I am lucky to have received some favorite ornaments and decorations from many family members. The ones that mean the most to me don't have much financial value, but they have tons of emotional value. Whether they're the ornaments that were on my first tree decorated by my brother or my nana's choirboy candles, these objects give me comfort, connection, and continuity at the holidays. Most recently my mom gave me a ceramic boot painted by her friend Ellie. It was part of our Christmas decor for as long as I can remember. I am proud to have it now, and each time I see it, I tap into a ton of happy memories.

I have many more things that didn't actually belong to my family but resemble ones that did, like many of the cardboard decorations and blow molds I've found at flea markets. Using them sparks joy in me, and I love sharing that joy with others.

3. Make, bake, or mail something.

My mom and sister are master bakers. Therefore, I wind up being the grateful recipient of many goodies. I don't do much holiday baking, but this year I did make my sister's chocolate tea bread for friends and family. (I included a copy of the recipe.)

I also send out many greeting cards. I typically use vintage cards, and because many were used, I mount them on new blank cards meant for a family photo. I also buy unused vintage cards when I see them and send those as well. On all the envelopes, I affix vintage holiday seals to add the quintessential Very Vintage Christmas touch.

For my decorations, I use dried oranges, strung popcorn, and cranberries for one of my trees. It's another mindful vintage activity that transports me to my childhood and looks so lovely when it's all done.

4. Give your time and be present.

Since I really think of Christmas as about five weeks rather than one day, I build in lots of little visits and gift exchanges over the course of that time frame. Visiting was part of our family's lifestyle growing up, and people just dropped by all the time. The world has changed since then, and rarely do we just "pop in" on someone, but I do like to schedule at least one visit a week with a friend or loved one. Sometimes it's doing something together, like wrapping gifts or shopping; sometimes it's just sitting and exchanging presents or baked goods.

Another activity I enjoy is going on a walk or drive to look at the decorations in different neighborhoods. It doesn't take long, but it is a memory-making moment that I treasure.

5. Share a meal.

My family has a lot of special meals around the holidays, but my two favorites are Christmas brunch and Christmas dinner. For brunch, Mom and Sis make scrambled eggs with cream of chicken soup (an old magazine recipe my family adopted years ago) and sausage and apples like my nana used to make. She was Pennsylvania Dutch, so a savory/sweet combo was always on the menu. Holiday cookies are also prominently arranged on a platter; they are very much a part of the meal, which is followed by gift opening!

For dinner, my sister has been making a big lasagna and salad. We've had many different menu items over the years, from Cornish game hens to Greek spinach pie, but this one is nice because the result is delicious, and it doesn't take that much time. It means she doesn't have to spend all day in the kitchen, like she has been doing all season long, making cookies, etc.

6. Do something interactive.

After dinner we always play a game, and on Christmas it's often *Trivial Pursuit*. Since none of us are great at the sports category, we replace those questions with Christmas trivia questions from another game. My family also gives hints and helps one another when we play. It's not at all competitive, and I love that energy.

After that, we typically watch one of the newer classic films on my long list of holiday favorites: *A Christmas Story*. It taps into so much nostalgia and joy and really speaks directly to the inner child in all of us. We know most of the lines by heart, so at least one of us will shout "You'll shoot your eye out" or "Mommy's little piggie!" Laughter always ensues, and it is a lovely way to end the day.

A VERY VINTAGE CHRISTMAS DECORATING

While I can't fit all twenty of my trees in this chapter, I did include many of my favorites. Some look similar each year, but I always create different ones, often inspired by new-to-me vintage decorations I've found throughout the year.

Living Room

The living room is where I feature five decorated trees, including my largest live tree. Standing more than nine feet high, it's almost as wide as it is tall. I achieve this look by finding a much larger tree and cutting off several feet at the bottom. I then use all the extra greenery throughout my home.

Since red and green really are the callout colors of Christmas, I add a lot of red to this tree to play off the green pine needles, using giant vintage Shiny Brite balls that were likely produced for use in stores or other public places. I found all of them at an antiques shop I love near my mom's house.

On top I have a very special motion star that was part of an estate lot purchased from a woman who had many magical holiday treasures. The heat of one tiny light bulb inside makes the center part turn, and it cascades light around the top of the entire room. When I plug it in each year, I think of its original owner with gratitude.

The flocked white tree is new and conveniently pre-lit. (Hear my sigh of relief for that after I get done stringing thousands of tiny white lights on the big live one!) On this tree I showcase some of my very favorite American ornaments made in the 1940s by the Corning Glass Company. Each is super silvered and hand-painted with vivid brushstrokes. On top I place a simple plastic light-up American star. Around the base I fashioned a tree skirt out of some wonderful vintage fabric given to me by my friend Daryl. In many ways it is a patriotic tree, because these were some of the very

Bob's Christmas Movie Picks

Since I listed some of my favorite classic holiday films in *A Very Vintage Christmas*, including ones I've mentioned already in this chapter, here are three more contemporary classics I watch and greatly enjoy every year.

CHRISTMAS VACATION

In my humble opinion, this movie has earned its spot among the all-time greatest holiday classic films. The dysfunctional Griswold family is very relatable, and Chevy Chase as Clark is perfectly kooky and endearing at the same time. While the movie is hilarious, I find the scene where he's watching old home movies in the attic to be very touching.

A CHRISTMAS MEMORY

I've heard this story by Truman Capote called "achingly beautiful," and I agree with that description. This one falls under the tearjerker category, and while there are two versions, I prefer the one from 1997 with Patty Duke. It tells the story of a special relationship between a young boy and his cousin, who is many years his senior. I've had relationships like this with my nana and others, so it hits close to home.

THE FAMILY STONE

With a magnificent cast and a gorgeous New England location, this movie carries both the zaniness of *Christmas Vacation* and the heartwarming nature of *A Christmas Memory*. I both laugh out loud and cry out loud every year when I watch it. While each character has lots of flaws, they all have hearts of gold. It's a family! And while a few of the plot lines might be considered farfetched by some, I'm all-in every year.

first ornaments the United States produced as WWII broke out. Americans wanted American ornaments, and these were the ones many homes had at the time.

My vintage RCA television sets *A Very Vintage Christmas* mood as I play a DVD of the yule log (when I'm not watching classic movies on it). It crackles and pops like a real fire and plays classic Christmas music. I grew up with a similar yule log on the TV at my grandparents' home, and it became a tradition to have it on in the background while we visited and exchanged gifts. I find it brings that comfort, connection, and continuity right to the heart of my holiday home.

The trees around the TV feature bubble lights, which are so magical and nostalgic. I love having them in this spot so I can enjoy watching them along with the TV!

Pro tip: As with all my items that use vintage lights, I use a dimmer on them to extend the life of the bulbs.

The bubble light display continues on the mantle, where I showcase them in a candolier. I love having them in front of the mirror, as it doubles the fun. I added greens and some cut flowers in vintage gold vases that reflect the lights. In front of the mantle, I placed two vintage candles I found at my local flea market. I love their size and details like the wooden base, created to look like an old-time candleholder. Like all vintage lighted items I own, I rewired them to ensure they were safe as well as beautiful.

With all the trees and the smaller lighted decorations, the whole room is illuminated by the soft glow of vintage Christmas, and it is my favorite place to wrap gifts, write out Christmas cards, and have quiet, contemplative times. It's also where we exchange gifts, and that comforting yule log and holiday music provide as much joy as they did in my childhood Christmases.

Sitting Room

Beyond the pocket doors of my living room is another room with the same size and layout. It's where I have my vintage RCA stereo, which I found at a yard sale many years ago. While I play records all year long, it is especially magical and comforting at the holidays, when I play all my favorite vintage albums (like those wonderful Firestone ones we all remember).

Next to the stereo, I decorated another pre-lit flocked tree. On it I added mostly antique European blown-glass ornaments in red, gold, and green. I placed the tree in a vintage decorative American stand, and on top I placed another vintage American star. This mix of European and American ornaments and decorations was very common in many homes, and for that reason, I love it.

On the opposite side of the room, I have the exact same pre-lit flocked tree, but it has a completely different look because of the ornaments I chose. They are all un-silvered American ornaments from the later years of WWII. It's another one I consider patriotic. Because the silvering typically used on these ornaments (like the ones on the white tree in the living room) was rationed for the war effort, these ornaments lack that mirrored finish. To

compensate, they were painted very joyful colors. On the flocked tree, they almost look like candy. Many have paper caps, as even the metal on the top was eventually removed.

I love the metaphor that when the things that made ornaments sparkle were gone, the artists compensated by dialing up the joy with paint. Christmas comes every year, and especially in war time, people needed joy.

On top of the WWII tree, I have another motion topper. This one is an angel and has a little propeller that sits atop the light bulb and cascades light around the room. In front of the tree, I have a vintage Howard Gale Santa Claus store display. He was made for 7UP and is a very jolly fellow, perched upon his original cardboard chimney. Also in the vicinity, I have another large metal candle that adds another pop of joy to the space.

Dining Room

My dining room has lots of green and gold accents, so I wanted the decorations to have the same colorway and feel more homespun and natural than the ones in other rooms.

The tree in the corner, while artificial, has a very natural look. I added new white lights and decided to decorate it with dried orange slices and strings of popcorn and cranberries like I used to make with my mom. To add some sparkle, I added a few antique blown-glass grape clusters in green and gold, along with antique glass fairy lights in the same colors. Inside each I place an LED tea light with a timer. These were originally made to hold a real candle and is how many lit their trees in the late 1800s. The tea lights are a way I found to get the same look without any safety concerns. I put the whole tree in a basket and topped it with a handmade glittered star. A bowl of fruit, a candle, and a lovely handmade owl tile by the late, great Laird Plumleigh complete the display.

On the large buffet, I used the same pre-lit artificial tree I have decorated for other holidays. This year I decided to pay homage to one of my favorite states: Vermont. Beautiful in every season, Vermont is especially magical in early winter, when you're quite likely to have a white Christmas.

I anchored the tree in a vintage sap bucket I found in a favorite antiques store in the Green Mountain State. Around the base I assembled greens (cut from the excess of my big tree in the living room), and in front of it I placed another vintage bubble light candolier with gold lights. Above the tree, along the top of the mirror, I added swags of greens with pinecones; on it I strung vintage Italian lanterns. I continued stringing them on the tree to add continuity.

For decorations I used handmade vintage needlepoint dollhouse rugs with bucolic New England scenes. My sister added a gold loop to the top of each so I could hang them easily. To top it all off, I hung glass icicles all over the display. If you're going to be in Vermont in the winter, you'll see lots of icicles! So while I was not in Vermont for Christmas, a little of Vermont was with me! Just to really set the mood, I played the great song "Moonlight in Vermont" when I unveiled this one. (I prefer the version by Margaret Whiting.)

Kitchen

They say the kitchen is the heart of a home, and like my heart, I want my kitchen to be happy. I can't think of any happier holiday decoration than those peppy knee-hugging pixies everyone seemed to have in the 1960s and 1970s.

I started off by lighting a green feather tree I've used for other holidays with "Lighted Ice" bulbs I found over the summer at a yard sale. With such fun, punchy colors, they remind me of those snow cones I had as a kid, and they set the mood for joy. I added vintage spinner ornaments that move with the warmth of the light bulbs. My family had these in the window of our business, and they are a direct callout to happy childhood memories for me. For a topper I used yet another lighted motion decoration. Santa and his sleigh rotate around the back so that he continually flies over the rooftops of the homes.

Once all of that was in place, I piled on the pixies. I put them both on and under the tree. On either side, I place a vintage blow mold, typically made for outdoor displays, but I like the impact they have when used inside. From the vintage light-up stars at the very top of the wall to the bottlebrush trees and elves at the base, this display makes me smile every morning while I'm having my coffee.

DE-TRIMMING

A lot of people ask me if I keep my
Christmas trees up all year long, and
the answer is no. I decorate trees for
almost every holiday, as you've seen
in this book, so technically some of
the actual trees remain. I decorate
them with different decor, but the
bottom line is that those twenty
trees are dismantled after Epiphany.

When I do this, it is a lot of
work—and yet another exercise in
mindfulness. I am far from a perfect
packer, but I do try to ensure my
decorations are safe for another
year; I use lots of acid-free tissue
and sturdy bins and boxes.

I am not super keen on tree
trimming parties because I'm
too much of a Christmas control
freak, but I think having a de-
trimming party is a great idea! I
would love help taking it all down;
unfortunately, everyone seems to be
busy that week!

That little tangent reminds me of a time I came home from college and put up three giant trees.
They were beautiful and showcased our vintage, handmade, and newly purchased ornaments.
After Christmas, however, I went back to college and left the trees for Mom to take down. Needless
to say, she was not happy about it. She said she was packing ornaments for weeks—and has never
let me hear the end of it.

In short, taking down trees isn't nearly as fun as putting them up, but I just put in a good movie
(or two or three or six or seven) and get the job done.

As a kid, I would actually take out all the Christmas boxes from the attic every July and take
inventory. That's another one of those "my son is crazy" stories my mom loves to tell. As an adult,
I no longer do a midyear inventory, but I do continue to find and collect all year long. In fact, that's
what the next chapter is all about!

Hanukkah

I mentioned earlier in the book that my partner, Sefton, is Jewish. He also grew up celebrating Christmas, so my decorations are not unfamiliar to him. Still, it is important to honor his family's faith and traditions and to carve out a space to celebrate them.

The primary decoration for Hanukkah is the menorah, where one candle is lit for each of the eight nights of the celebration. There are actually nine candles, but the middle one is used to light the others. Often referred to as the "festival of lights," Hanukkah is a joyful holiday I am now excited to celebrate. It honors a miracle of a lamp staying lit despite the odds. Since I believe in miracles and always root for the underdog, I love this holiday!

Each night we light an additional candle and sing two Hebrew prayers (I am still working on the proper pronunciation of all the words!) and enjoy a mindful, connected moment. We also give small gifts like chocolate coins (called gelt) and play with a top called a dreidel (while of course singing "The Dreidel Song").

It is often during these times that I not only learn more about Sefton's faith and customs but also his childhood. Like with all holidays, engaging in these activities brings back memories we get to share with others.

Since Hanukkah happens at the same time the house is decorated for Christmas, I try to carve out one spot for lighting the menorah. We typically do this in the kitchen because that's where Sefton lit the menorah as a kid. Also, the marble counter is a more wax-friendly surface, should there be any dripping.

This year I found a beautiful vintage menorah at a local thrift shop. I've placed it in a favorite corner, flanked by two paintings of deer that I absolutely love. Since the classic color of Hanukkah is blue, I added blue candles and placed it on a blue flowered tablecloth.

I feel that it's one of my most elegant displays, especially because it's so simple. Among all the razzle-dazzle of my Christmas decorations, it really is a standout. I love the way the lit candles reflect in the glass of the framed watercolors.

I use some electric menorahs as well. Like many light-up holiday decorations, they are both kitschy and sweet at the same time. Instead of lighting candles, you just screw in an additional light bulb for each night. I typically place these in the windows. After Hanukkah ends, I like to leave them lit for the rest of the holiday season.

The menorah is central to the Hanukkah celebration. On the first night, one candle is lit; each subsequent night, one more is added, for eight nights. The middle candle is called the shamash and it is used to light the others. Dreidels are spun, latkes are made, and gifts are given. Known as the festival of lights, it is a greatly joyful holiday.

I love vintage handmade objects. Someone many decades ago fashioned this tree out of paint stirrers painted green. All of the wonderful miniature decorations were likely found at a craft store. I remember buying many objects like this when I was a kid.

Rudolph comes in many incarnations, and I love this vintage plastic one.

It's never too early to start saving for
Christmas gifts, as this sweet hearth
bank reminds us.

Santa is taking your calls! I purchased
this vintage wind-up toy Santa from
his original owner. She was happy to
share that he still works.

This vintage Santa candy box has
wonderful details. I love the icicles
along the top of the chimney.

Bottlebrush trees are very nostalgic
for many. This white one with glass
beads is a favorite of mine.

Light-up ceramic trees like this one are among the most nostalgic vintage holiday decorations out there. Everyone seemed to have one of these (or two or three).

I collect vintage Christmas planters like this one featuring carolers. I like to add a bottlebrush tree or two to the back where the plant was supposed to go.

This cute elf was one of Hallmark's original ornaments back in 1973.

Because it is so lightweight, Styrofoam was a great material for holiday decor. This giant Santa head is easy to hang and makes a big statement.

One of my favorite images of Old St. Nick, this standup cardboard decoration is one of a pair. They were made for store displays, and I love the vibrant colors and details.

Another lightweight Santa decoration, this plastic Santa in a holly wreath looks great just about anywhere.

Someone long ago thought the box that held their Christmas cards was too nice to throw away. I agree.

Firestone records are among my very favorites. Everyone had them and played them. My family sure did. I love displaying them as well as listening to them.

Joyful American ornaments like these look great on any tree or just displayed in the box.

Music is central to Christmas. My record player is going all season long, and these three albums are on most frequently.

The minute I start to hear "The Little Drummer Boy" for the first time each year, I get a little weepy.

Elvis adds soul to any holiday setting.

John Denver and The Muppets' *A Christmas Together* is my all-time favorite Christmas album.

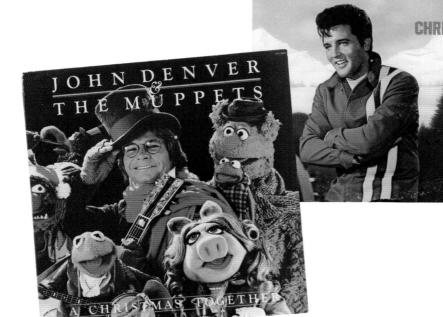

I collect December issues of vintage magazines because they are filled with wonderful entertaining and decorating ideas as well as really fun ads. My partner found this one for me at an estate sale.

These knee-hugger elves were everywhere in midcentury holiday home decor. I decorated a whole tree with them in my kitchen.

Vintage Sears catalogs contain a treasure trove of nostalgia. I love paging through them to see the original prices on my now vintage holiday decorations.

Light-up blow mold decorations come in all shapes and sizes. I love this reindeer lounging on a chimney top. Similarly, I think this Santa perched on a fireplace is a hoot.

This antique celluloid St. Nicholas has a spring connecting his head to his body, so he bobbles in addition to looking cool.

Vintage handmade objects are my favorites. I love this round wooden sign, which was likely made for a store.

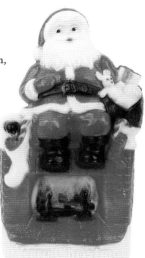

This handmade child's calendar includes several red-letter days, including Christmas.

∗◈∙----------------------∙◈∗

Vintage tins like this one have wonderful graphics and are great for both display and storage. I keep my ornament hooks in one.

∗◈∙----------------------∙◈∗

A forest of red plastic trees looks great just about anywhere. These were probably originally intended to go with a train display.

Cool pieces of holiday ephemera like this child's play catch my eye at flea markets all year long.

A vintage copy of Rudolph makes a great addition to any holiday display and is worth an annual read.

This fun Father Christmas horn doubles as a decoration.

Nobody does it like Bing Crosby! I love displaying the album cover and listening to the record.

Vintage Christmas cards have wonderful graphics. I love the simplicity of the holly plant card and the sheer beauty of the one featuring the candles. A new card made for me by my friend Sharon is already a classic in my collection.

I have versions of this bubble light candolier all over my home. Each one gives off a magical holiday glow.

Holiday Cheer

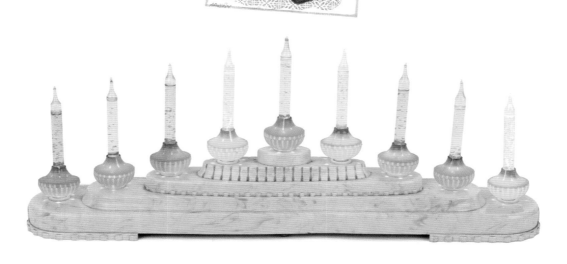

Everyone knows Coke had great images of Santa Claus. When Pepsi wanted to feature him, they hired Norman Rockwell, who created this jolly fellow.

•❖•--•❖•

This large light-up plastic Santa decoration adds fun wherever he's displayed.

•❖•--•❖•

Many antique ornaments like this have lost their color over the years. I call them my "Velveteen Rabbit" ornaments because, to me, they are more beautiful because they've been loved.

This midcentury iron candle tree is a fun and uncommon piece of vintage holiday decor.

One of many ceramic elves in my collection, this fellow is particularly joyful.

A kitschy-cute 1960s angel tree topper.

This happy vintage felt reindeer looks great with a flock of his fellows or on his own.

A box of post-WWII hand-painted American ornaments

This Italian soldier ornament looks dazzling on my largest tree.

A box of rare 1960s Polish indent ornaments with cute plastic figures inside.

This tiny vintage toy train has its original key and still works.

Finding Vintage
HOLIDAY ITEMS

As a kid, I was never sad or let down the day after Christmas. Why? Because that's when Mom and I used to hit all the sales on holiday decorations. We'd hit them—and we'd hit them hard! Up bright and early on December 26, we'd make our way to Hess's, our hometown department store, and dive into the 50-percent-off party. We'd come home with bags of magical baubles and add them to our already decorated holiday home. Such happy memories. I still have many of those ornaments and decorations from our shopping sprees; now, of course, they are vintage!

What lesson did this little tradition teach me? Shop after the holiday at hand, and you can buy more for less. I've expanded that cardinal rule of thumb to one of my standby catchphrases for finding vintage holiday items: "Buy off-season and save!"

Like all the things I use to decorate my home, I find most of my vintage holiday decor at flea markets, tag sales, thrift stores, and other vintage venues. The very best advice I can give for those who want to start collecting and decorating is to buy off-season. In other words, don't look for vintage Halloween in September but in April, when demand is lower and so are the prices.

Just as in retail settings where new things are sold, like the ones my mom and I shopped, holiday items are obviously more expensive around the time of that actual holiday. I typically find my best vintage Christmas items in the summer and my best vintage Easter items in the fall.

While I shop many antiques stores, thrift shops, yard sales, estate sales, and auctions, my primary shopping grounds for finding vintage holiday items are flea markets. Since many of these vendors liquidate estates, they typically have holiday items available for sale all year long.

Here are my favorite flea markets for finding vintage holiday items year-round.

BLAKE DUMMOND AND DANIEL YUND

BLAKE DUMMOND AND DANIEL YUND

BOB'S TOP 10 US FLEA MARKETS FOR VINTAGE HOLIDAY ITEMS

1. Burlington, Kentucky
Burlington Antique Show
burlingtonantiqueshow.com

2. Cumming, Georgia
Lakewood 400 Antiques Market
lakewoodantiques.com

3. Brimfield, Massachusetts
Brimfield Antiques Show
https://brimfieldantiqueshows.com

4. Canton, Texas
Canton Trade Days
firstmondaycanton.com

5. Chicago, Illinois
Randolph Street Market
randolphstreetmarket.com/
chicagoantiquemarket/

6. Lambertville, New Jersey
The Golden Nugget
http://gnflea.com

7. New Milford, Connecticut
The Elephant's Trunk
etflea.com

8. Philadelphia, Pennsylvania
The Philly Flea
philafleamarkets.org

9. Springfield, Ohio
Springfield Antiques Show and
Flea Market
springfieldantiqueshow.com

10. Kutztown, Pennsylvania
Renninger's Extravaganza
renningers.net

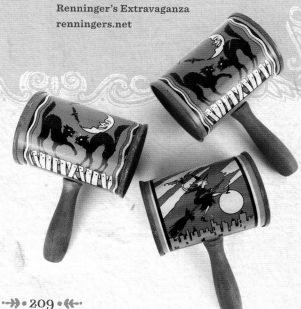

Pay It Forward

PASS ALONG DECORATIONS, TRADITIONS, RECIPES, AND MORE

If you've read this book so far and come to this chapter, you know I'm shamelessly sentimental about objects from the past. My very favorite items are ones I've been given by family members like my grandmothers and my mom. They've passed along their favorite holiday finds to me, and now when I decorate with them, I am literally tapping into that comfort, connection, and continuity I've talked about throughout this book.

These items hold emotional value and thus are very important to me. Of course, many items I have are not family pieces, but many remind me of ones my family had when I was a kid. I always say that even if something didn't belong to your family but is similar and brings back good memories, then that is what it's all about.

In *A Very Vintage Christmas*, I talk about how many times I have been to estate sales where I've found wonderful holiday items that were lovingly packed away. The owners didn't realize that the last time they packed them away, it would literally be the last time. So I always encourage everyone I know to give away some of their favorite holiday items while they are still alive to see someone else enjoying them.

My family does this. It's a way of creating new memories with old things. And when someone passes, it's not up to me to take something, because it was already given to me.

The same goes for that bowl that always holds the mashed potatoes at Thanksgiving or the ceramic jack-o'-lantern that is on the dining room buffet every year. Passing along these objects helps to pass along love—from one generation to another; from one friend to another.

My grandmother's Father Christmas ornament is always front and center on my largest tree.

Now might be a good time for me to mention that I hear from people all the time who say, "My kids don't want my stuff." Tastes and lifestyles change with the generations. There are things that younger people might not want, and that's okay. Chances are those things are furniture, decorative pieces, collections, etc. But when it comes to vintage holiday items, I think you'll find the emotional connection is much greater. So while your kids might not want your dining room table, they will probably want at least some of your Christmas ornaments.

A miracle is a shift in perception. So perhaps you offer your vintage holiday items to the next generation and see what they have to say. If they remember them from their childhood Christmas tree or front door, they will have emotional value, and that goes a long way.

The younger generations also place great emphasis on reducing their carbon footprint. I always say there's nothing greener than using what already exists! So instead of buying new Halloween decorations, they might really like the idea of using ones that not only have sentimental value but also were not just recently mass-produced.

Start a conversation with kids and grandkids about what they want (versus what you might want them to want); you might be pleasantly surprised at what you'll be able to pass along. When you do, consider adding a note that says where the Thanksgiving platter was purchased or what was served on it. Why not even include a recipe?

Aside from actual objects, I believe that passing along traditions is equally important. I took over the stocking stuffing when Mom gave me the Christmas stockings my brother made for us. And sometimes you don't even need an object to pass along vintage ways that are associated with a family member. For example, every time I decorate a tree for the birds and squirrels in my backyard with nuts and pinecones rolled in peanut butter and birdseed, I am channeling the love and kindness of my nana. When I do things like this, her kindness lives on in this world.

Similarly, my mom and sister made me a cookbook of family recipes so that I can begin to make them and share them with others, just as they've shared them with me my whole life.

In this chapter I'm happy to share with you some recipes my mom passed along to me. All are closely associated with holidays, so they are even more meaningful to me. I chose to share the recipes as my mom (and my nana) wrote them. I love seeing their writing, as it automatically helps me to feel close to them. Long live the handwritten recipe card! What wonderful family heirlooms to pass along! Why not consider writing a few of your favorites this year and giving them as gifts? My mom often gave the recipe for a baked good along with the actual item she'd made. It's a very vintage and heartfelt gift!

I hope you try a few, and that they bring you joy and are a treat for your taste buds. It's my way of passing along some love to each and every one of you.

Remember, cooking for others really is an expression of love, just like anything you make for someone, whether it be a card, a wreath, or an ornament. So in the spirit of all holidays, give from your heart and share with others; chances are you'll be happy—and they'll be happy too.

Nana's nut thins are a yearly Christmas favorite. Mom's spiced tongues are treats at Halloween and Christmas.

Spiced Tongues

350° 10-12 min

2 cups sugar
1½ cups margerine
2 eggs
8 tblsp. molasses (½ cup)
5 cups flour
2 tsp. ginger
3 tsp. cinnamon
2 tsp. cloves
4 scant tsp baking soda

Make a small ball — then shape like a hot dog about 2½ inches long. Roll in granulated sugar. Do not place too close together on cookie sheet. Cookies will be soft but will get crisp as they cool. Enjoy!

Christmas Nut Thins

1 cup butter — 1 cup sugar
1½ cup unbleached flour.
2 eggs — 1 cup chopped nuts
1 tsp Vanilla — ½ tsp salt

Blend sugar & butter together add well beaten eggs. Sift in flour & salt — add nuts add vanilla — mix until smooth & light —
Drop on greased baking sheet
Bake in moderate oven (375) about 10 minutes

I love having Mom's and Nana's recipes in their handwriting.

Mom's Spiced Tongues (see previous page) are a powerful taste of home for me. We have them at both Halloween and Christmas.

Nana's Nut Thins (see previous page) have been a Christmas staple in our family for generations.

Whenever I go to someone's home, I like to bring fresh flowers (from my garden if possible) in a vintage vase.

214

I readily use vintage cards like this one in my holiday decorating; I especially like using ones that came from family members so I can see their handwriting inside.

Dying Easter eggs with onion skins is an old family tradition. These were done by my sister Robin. Pro Tips: Boil skins until water is a deep reddish brown. Add eggs and boil thirteen more minutes. Remove from heat and add ice cubes to stop eggs from cooking. Dry them and polish with cooking oil for a beautiful shine.

One of Mom's dearest friends, Ellie, made her this boot in ceramics class in the 1970s. It was always part of our holiday decor. Now Mom passed it along to me, so I can enjoy it.

Vintage serving dishes like this one are great to both use and display. They are often handed down from one generation to the next and have great meaning to us.

•◦•-------------------------------•◦•

My fourth grade teacher was Jewish, and she took delight in sharing her favorite traditions with us. One was making potato latkes at Hanukkah. I still have the recipe in my eight-years-old handwriting.

Bobby Richter
Potato Latkes (pancakes

2½ cups of raw grated potatoes
4 tablespoons of grated onion
1 teaspoon of salt
2 large eggs
3 tablespoons of breadcrumbs
pepper to taste

Directions
1. Peel the potatoes
2. Grate the potatoes
3. Grate or chop the onions
4. Mix the pot
5. Beat the eggs in a little bowl
6. Pour them in with the potatoes and onion
7. Pour in the salt
8. Pour in the breadcrumbs
9. Stir everything well
10. Heat the frying pan
11. Melt some butter in the pan
12. Add some oil. Let it get hot
13. Drop some batter in the pan

with a spoon and flatten with the spoon.
14. Fry it until it is crisp and brown on both sides
15 Eat! (You can put apple sauce or sour cream on them

My friend Jean made me this wonderful Valentine's Day card from salvaged sheet music and parts of an old discarded book. I treasure it.

- -

Mom makes this chocolate cake for just about everyone's birthday. It remains one of my all-time favorites.

DREAMS ARE THE SOUL'S PANTRY. KEEP IT WELL STOCKED AND YOUR SOUL WILL NEVER HUNGER.

CINDY WILLIAMS

Recipe from the ♥

Cooking Time: Chocolate Cake

2 cups flour
2 " sugar
⅓ cup oil
1 " coffee
¾ cup cocoa   1 tsp. baking powder
1 tsp vanilla   2 tsp. " soda
1 cup milk   ¼ " salt
2 eggs
    Blend tog. sugar, eggs
+ oil. In separate bowl, mix baking
powder, baking soda, cocoa + coffee.
    Add remaining ingred. + mix
                              (over)

until smooth. Bake in 9 x 13
pan @ 350° for 30 min.

Peanut Butter Icing.

1 lb. xxx sugar
½ cup shortening (butter)
3 tbsp milk
⅔ cup peanut butter

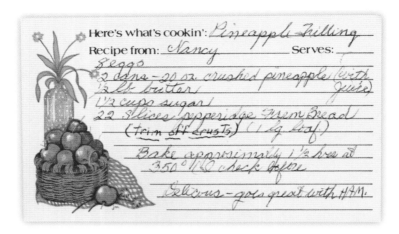

Here's what's cookin': *Pineapple Filling*
Recipe from: *Nancy*   Serves:

8 eggs
2 cans - 20 oz. crushed pineapple (with juice)
1/2 lb butter
1 1/2 cups sugar
22 slices Pepperidge Farm Bread
   (trim off crusts) (1 lg loaf)

Bake approximately 1 1/2 hrs at
350° M check before

Delicious - goes great with HAM.

Easter dinner at our house always includes pineapple filling. Here's the recipe Mom passed along to me. It goes great with ham.

For St. Patrick's Day Mom makes this potato candy. Biting into a piece takes me right back to childhood.

Here's what's cookin' *Potato Candy* Recipe from the kitchen of _____

1 small potato
Dash of salt
1 Tbsp butter
1 lb 10x sugar
1 tsp. vanilla
1/3 cup peanut butter
   Peel cooked potato.
Mash with salt + butter. Add
sugar 1/2 at a time, beating
until smooth & well blended.
Mix in the vanilla - If mixture is not stiff enough   Serves ____

to roll- add more sugar.
   Roll out between 2 sheets of wax
paper until 1/8 inch thick. Spread with
peanut butter. Roll up like a jelly roll. Chill
for 1 hr., then slice into 1/4" pieces. Let
ripen a day before eating.

Blueberry Muffins ②

1/4 cup butter (4 Tbsp.) & 3/4 c. sugar - cream
1 egg   — add beat well
2 cups flour
1/2 tsp salt   } add this mixture
2 Tsp. b. powder   alternately with 1/2 c. milk
  Fold in 1 cup blueberries + top
with combination of 1/2 cup sugar - 1/4 c. butter
       1/3 cup flour + 1/2 tsp. cinn.
Carol R.   400° - 20 - 25 min. (over)

—Joyce

Crumbs
1 cup flour
1/4 " sugar
1/2 of 1/4 lb butter
1/2 tsp. salt.

shake blueberries with a little flour before adding to batter.

Salmon Party Log

1 – 1 lb can (2 cups) red salmon
1 8 oz pkg. cream cheese (softened)
1 Tbsp lemon juice
2 tsp grated onion
1 tsp prepared horseradish
1/4 tsp. salt
1/4 " liquid smoke
1/2 cup chopped pecans
     3 Tbsp chopped parsley

Drain + flake salmon
removing skin + bones.

Combine salmon with next 6 ing's.
Mix thoroughly. Chill several hours.
Combine nuts + parsley. Shape salmon
mixture in 8×2" log. Roll in nut
mixture. Chill well + serve
with crackers.
  (I always made it in the
shape of a ball.)

4th of July perfectly coincides with blueberry season. As such, Mom bakes these blueberry muffins as part of our celebration.

New Year's Eve in our house is about celebrating with family. Every year, Mom makes this savory treat. Hers always looks like a ball rather than a log, and it tastes great, served with crackers.

Mom framed this photo of me on Santa's lap in this cute holiday frame. For years, I saw it on display in her home and a few years ago, she gave it to me.

Thanksgiving wouldn't be complete without Mom's pumpkin custard (see page 158). It's lighter than regular pumpkin pie and is my favorite holiday dessert. We always serve it with fresh homemade whipped cream.

Bake 10 min @ 450° — reduce heat to 350° + bake until knife comes out clean.

My Favorite Recipe

Pumpkin Custard

Mix Tog: 1 tsp. cinnamon

from: ¼ tsp. nutmeg   serves:

pinch salt

½ cup brown sugar + ⅓ cup granulated sugar

Separate 2 eggs to 2 cups pumpkin.

Add dry ingred. & 2 cups milk

3 Tbsp. (optional) Whiskey &

stiffly beaten egg whites.

Pour into unbaked pie shell

(over)

This vintage Seder plate has seen many Passover celebrations. These objects have great emotional value when passed down from one generation to the next.

Mom's made these muffins for my birthday for many years. Part of the joy of a summertime birthday is getting to have things that use fresh fruits and vegetables.

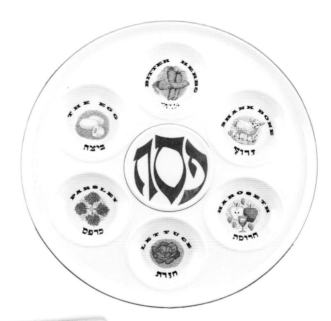

Here's what's cookin': Peach Muffins
Recipe from: Anna Marie   Serves: 24

2 cups sifted all purpose flour
½ tsp salt
1 Tbsp. baking powder
3/4 cup granulated sugar
1 egg
1 cup milk
4 tbsp. melted butter (½ stick)
1½ to 2 cups diced fresh peaches

Preheat oven to 425° F. Sift flour, salt, b.p. + sugar together in bowl. Beat egg well - add milk + melted butter. Then add liquid to flour. Stir with a wooden spoon just enough to combine ingredients. Don't overmix!

Peel + dice fresh ripe peaches about the size of sugar cubes + fold into batter. Pour batter into well-greased muffin tins, filling each cup about ⅔'s full. Bake about 18-20 minutes or until muffins are nicely browned. If you can find the 5 oz. pyrex cups used for popovers - they can also be used to make spectacular muffins. Approx. 5 doz.

Acknowledgments

A Very Vintage Holiday is an expression of my enthusiasm for the magical times of the year we set aside for celebration. To the generations who came before me and made these holidays special, thank you.

Thank you to Mom and my sister Robin, who have cooked, baked, made, and wrapped countless extraordinary creations over the years. I am in awe of your talent, your tireless work, and your genuine holiday spirt. Because of you, every holiday is beautiful and memorable.

As shared on the pages of this book, my home is very much decorated for all the holidays. An enormous thank-you to Sefton, my partner, for supporting my vision and navigating a house filled with thousands of ornaments, lights, and decorations with grace and love. With you, Sefton, every day is a holiday (*literally and figuratively!*). And thanks, too, for your excellent proofreading skills. You've got brains as well as beauty!

For my dear, talented friend Sharon Dellapiazza: Thank you for creating magical works of art you so generously gift to me; thank you for doing my Halloween makeup and costumes; most of all, thank you for being a constant cheerleader and companion on the joyride of life. Our friendship is truly vintage and filled with laughter and love.

Another amazing friend who has contributed to my work in countless ways, Renee Soto, thank you for so many things; the list goes on and on. It includes restoring beautiful broken objects, making St. Patrick's Day ornaments, building my websites, and proofreading this book. You truly are a Renaissance woman!

Christopher Radko, my dear friend and mentor, thank you for writing such a heartfelt foreword to another of my books! Most of all, thank you for always believing in me. Your light keeps getting brighter the more you shine it.

Bud Hayman, the photographer who captured the beautiful images in this book, is both wildly talented and a lot of fun. Bud, my friend and colleague, thank you for showing up to all the shoots with great energy and a commitment to making each image a magnificent one. Mission accomplished!

To Blake Drummond and Daniel Yund, who contributed some additional key photography, such as my author photo and others, including favorite shopping venues, thank you. You are deeply talented photographers and true friends.

To other extraordinary friends and supporters—Jay Kumar, Kelly Dotson, Mary Margaret Frederick, Christina and Chuck McNamee, Mollie Middleton, Kim Black, Amy Coss, Daryl Lynn O'Connell, Peggy Damm, and Matt Geraldi—thank you for your omnipresent love and light. I am so grateful to you!

All my vintage holiday collections continue to grow and flourish because of the amazing antiques dealer friends who find treasures for me all year long. It's impossible to thank all of you, but here's a short list: Bea, Julia, Renee, Tony, Jay, Frank, Murat, Robert, Erica, Chanelle, Lisa, Stacey, Armand, Evelyn, Bruce, Bill, Joanne, Darlene, Tori, Alan, Herb, Jean, Marge, Scott, Dolores, and Michele. Thank you!

To my friends at Good Stuff Thrift—Eva, David, Jill, Brett, Kim, Saralynn, and all the many wonderful volunteers—thank you! So many of the beautiful decorations in this book came from your magical stores.

Thank you to my pal Claudia at NOVA Thrift for all the treasures you've found for me.

A big thanks to my old friend Andy Eckoff at Bountiful Acres for always ensuring I get the biggest, best trees.

And to Eric Horsnall at Finkle's Hardware, thank you for your patient, expert rewiring of my bubble light trees so they can continue to be a magical presence in my home.

For Meg and Dave Pierson, thank you for your magical work at Vintage Vibe. The 1947 RCA you refurbished has brought much joy to my home and to the pages of this book.

Of course, to my team at Globe, thank you, Amy Lyons, David LeGere, Meredith Dias, Wendy Reynolds, Steph Scott, Diana Nuhn, and Cooper Filhaber for helping me bring this book into fruition.

And last but certainly not least, to those loved ones who've left this physical world, your spirit is very much alive in my work and my energy. Johnny, Nana, Eve, Lily, Teresa, Dad, Grandma, Walter, Julie Tante, and Sunny; thank you for helping me become the guy who loves holidays—and just wrote a book all about it.

THANK YOU!

About the Author

As America's Vintage Lifestyle Expert, **Bob Richter** focuses on tapping into the best of the past while living today. He is known to TV audiences as "The Designer" on the PBS series *Market Warriors*, where he traveled the country one flea market at a time, finding beautiful objects and meeting beautiful people. On a global level, Bob hosts *Flea Market Minute*, where he visits markets and shops in European cities including Paris, Budapest, Berlin, and Brussels and US cities like Los Angeles, Santa Fe, New York, and Alameda. Bob was also the host of *Minute Makeover* on ShelterPop, where he inexpensively transformed rooms at lightning speed.

Bob is the author of two previous books, *A Very Vintage Christmas* and *Vintage Living*: *A Very Vintage Holiday* taps into his love of the holidays and offers a sneak peek into his world of collecting and decorating, which began at the age of seven.

Regularly featured on *Good Morning America*, *TODAY*, and The Hallmark Channel, Bob is frequently profiled in print media outlets, including the *New York Times*, *Entertainment Weekly*, *Parade* magazine, the *Huffington Post*, the Associated Press, *Country Living*, and *Apartment Therapy*.

Bob grew up working for the family interior design business, which specialized in custom window treatments. There he began his appreciation of textile and color. Operating under the motto "Just a Shade better," the business was run by his grandmother, who trained Bob's eye and gave him a strong design vocabulary. She continues to be Bob's greatest inspiration.

As an interior designer and stylist, Bob turns ordinary spaces into magical environments that are a treat for the senses. His love of design has been ingrained in him since he was a latchkey kid in Allentown, Pennsylvania. Often "refreshing" his mother's house before she returned home from work, Bob got his inspirations from old movies and attic treasures. He began collecting antiques at the age of seven while tagging along with his older brother, thus beginning a lifelong love affair with garage sales, flea markets, and thrift shops.

BLAKE DUMMOND AND DANIEL YUND

At that same young age, Bob's father gave him a box of vintage Christmas ornaments and said, "It's time you started collecting something." Bob took that gift (and directive) literally and began his lifelong passion for vintage holiday decor. His collection continues to grow, and so does the number of trees he decorates. At last count, it was twenty, with more on the horizon.

As *A Very Vintage Holiday* showcases, Bob doesn't limit his collecting to vintage Christmas decorations. He shops and decorates for all holidays—Halloween, Easter, Valentine's Day, and more.

A Tastemaker on the high-end shopping portal *One Kings Lane*, Bob frequently hosts shopping events featuring vintage holiday items and other treasures from his vintage vault. When Bob's not out at a flea market, thrift shop, or other vintage venue, he's at home decorating (and redecorating) his historic home.

You can read more about Bob at richterdesign.net.

About the Photographer

Bud Hayman began his career as a videographer for QVC in 1996. In 2006 he created Bud Hayman Images LLC, working freelance for the past twenty years with an extensive list of clients. When he is not enjoying spending time with his family and two golden retrievers, often down in Avalon, New Jersey, Bud is a photographer of all trades: food, products, interiors, even video, ranging from pharmaceuticals to documentaries.

You will likely find Bud trying to make everyday objects capture your attention and look amazing, which is his goal for every project, large and small. Currently he is excited about working on a documentary for a rare disease and hopes it sheds some light on an interesting medical phenomenon.

Bud feels fortunate to be able to do the thing he loves every day and collaborate with some brilliant people. As most people will say, he always brings positive energy and light to the shoot. You can find his recent work at budhayman.com.